Eclipse IDE
Pocket Guide

Eclipse IDE
Pocket Guide

Ed Burnette

O'REILLY®

Beijing · Cambridge · Farnham · Köln · Paris · Sebastopol · Taipei · Tokyo

Eclipse IDE Pocket Guide
by Ed Burnette

Published by O'Reilly Media, Inc., 1005 Gravenstein Highway North,
Sebastopol, CA 95472.

O'Reilly books may be purchased for educational, business, or sales
promotional use. Online editions are also available for most titles
(*safari.oreilly.com*). For more information, contact our corporate/
institutional sales department: (800) 998-9938 or *corporate@oreilly.com*.

Editor:	Brett McLaughlin
Production Editor:	Marlowe Shaeffer
Cover Designer:	Ellie Volckhausen
Interior Designer:	David Futato

Printing History:

August 2005:   First Edition.

0-596-10065-5
[C]

Contents

Part IX. Help and Community

Appendix. Commands   83

PART I

Introduction

Welcome to the pocket guide for the Eclipse Integrated Development Environment. This book is the ultimate "no fluff" user's manual for the Eclipse IDE, in particular, its Java Development Toolkit (JDT). This book is designed to get you up and running quickly in the environment even if you've never used Eclipse before. Some Java™ programming knowledge will be helpful when reading this guide, but even if you're new to Java, you can still find a good deal of useful information within these pages. Let's begin with an overview of what Eclipse is and how to download and install it. If you're already using Eclipse, you can skip this section and jump to Part II.

What Is Eclipse?

Eclipse is an IDE for "anything, and nothing at all," meaning that it can be used to develop software in any language, not just Java. It started as a proprietary replacement for Visual Age for Java from IBM, but was open sourced in November 2001. Eclipse is now controlled by an independent nonprofit organization called the Eclipse Foundation. Since 2001, it has been downloaded over 50 million times; it is now being used by thousands of developers worldwide. It also has a sizable following in the university community, where it is used in classes on programming and object-oriented design.

Conventions Used in This Book

Italic
> Used for filenames, directory names, URLs, and tools from Unix such as *vi*. Also used for emphasis and to introduce new terms.

`Constant width`
> Used for names of Java packages, methods, etc.; commands; variables; and code excerpts.

`Constant width bold`
> Used for keywords within code examples and for text that the user should type literally.

System Requirements

Eclipse runs on today's most popular operating systems, including Windows XP, Linux, and Mac OS X. It requires Java to run, so if you don't already have Java installed on your machine, you must first install a recent version. You can download Java for Windows and Linux from *http://java.sun.com*; look for the J2SE SDK (Software Development Kit) package without a NetBeans™ bundle. Mac OS X has Java preinstalled. See Table 1 for the minimum and recommended system requirements.

Table 1. System requirements for Eclipse

Requirement	Minimum	Recommended
Java version	1.4.0	5.0 or greater
Memory	512 MB	1 GB or more
Free disk space	300 MB	1 GB or more
Processor speed	800 Mhz	1.5 Ghz or faster

In order to unpack Eclipse's download package, you will need a standard archive program. Some versions of Windows have one built in; for other versions, you can use a program such as WinZip (*http://www.winzip.com*). The other platforms come with an archive program preinstalled.

TIP

In the interests of space and simplicity, the rest of this book will focus on the Windows version of Eclipse. Other platforms will be very similar, although you may notice slight platform-specific differences.

Downloading Eclipse

To download the Eclipse IDE, go to *http://www.eclipse.org*. Click on "downloads" and then select the most recent stable or release version of the Eclipse SDK for your platform. If prompted for a mirror site, pick the one located closest to you. If that one is slow or unavailable, simply return to the download page and try a different mirror, or try the main site.

TIP

You may see other download packages such as Runtime, JDT, and RCP on the download page. You don't need those. Just get the one package called Eclipse SDK.

Installing Eclipse

First, install Java if you haven't already. Then download the Eclipse SDK to a temporary directory. Use your archive program to unpack Eclipse into a permanent directory. There are no setup programs and no registry values to deal with.

After you have unpacked the SDK, you should have a subdirectory called *eclipse*, which in turn has directories in it such as *plugins* and *features*. If you don't see these, check the settings on your archive program. A common mistake is to unpack Eclipse in such a way that its directory structure is not preserved. Eclipse won't run unless you unpack it with the exact directory paths that exist in the archive.

3, 2, 1, Launch!

You are now ready to launch Eclipse. Inside the *eclipse* directory, you'll find a launcher program for the IDE called, strangely enough, *eclipse* (or *eclipse.exe*). Invoke that program to bring up the IDE.

TIP

On Windows, you may find it convenient to create a desktop shortcut to launch Eclipse.

Specify a Workspace

The first time you start Eclipse, you will be prompted for the location of your workspace. The workspace is the location where your source code and other files and settings will be stored on your workstation. Specify a permanent location—somewhere *not* in your install directory—preferably a location that will be backed up regularly.

Putting the workspace in a different place from where you installed Eclipse makes upgrades easier. See the "Getting Upgrades" section, later in Part I, for more information.

Exploring Eclipse

When Eclipse starts up, you will be greeted with the Welcome screen (see Figure 1). This screen provides an introduction for new users who don't have the benefit of a pocket guide to Eclipse; for now you can skip over it by closing the

---

Welcome view (click on the close icon—the × next to the word "Welcome"). You can always come back to the Welcome screen later by selecting Welcome from the Help menu.

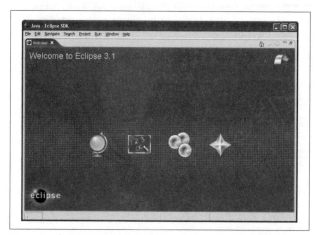

Figure 1. The Welcome screen allows you to explore introductory material, including examples and tutorials.

Getting Upgrades

Eclipse includes an automatic update facility that can handle *point releases* (i.e., bug-fix versions) without any work on your part. For example, Eclipse would install an upgrade from 3.1.0 to 3.1.1 automatically. However, for anything more substantial, the best practice is to do a manual clean install.

TIP

A clean install is especially important if you want to use beta versions of Eclipse (called *Stable* or *Milestone builds* on the download page). Milestone builds are sometimes buggy, so you may need to temporarily go back and run your previous version.

For example, let's say you have been running Version 3.1 for a while and now Version 3.2 has come out. You want to upgrade right away because each new release contains a number of important bug fixes and useful new features. Also, if you have a problem with an older release and report it to the developers, they will simply ask you to upgrade (see "Reporting Bugs" in Part IX). So, you should upgrade, but what's the best way to do it?

First, rename your *eclipse* directory to something else, like *eclipse3.1*. Then download the new SDK package and install it normally, as if you had never installed Eclipse before. This is called a *clean install* because you are not attempting to mix new and old code together. Note that your workspace doesn't need to change at all, but you should back it up before running the new version just in case. Now do you see why I recommended you don't keep your workspace in the install directory?

TIP

Any additional plug-ins you have installed for Eclipse will need to be reinstalled at this point unless you keep them in an *extension location* separate from the Eclipse SDK.

Moving On

Congratulations—you've successfully downloaded, installed, and started exploring Eclipse. In Part II, you'll learn what all the windows and buttons are for and how to set up the environment just the way you like it. If you want to skip ahead and start writing a Java program, jump to Part III.

Workbench 101

Eclipse's main window, called the *workbench*, is built with a few common user interface elements (see Figure 2). Learn how to use them and you can get the most out of the IDE. The two most important elements are views and editors. If you're already familiar with the Eclipse workbench, you can skim this section or skip to Part III to start programming.

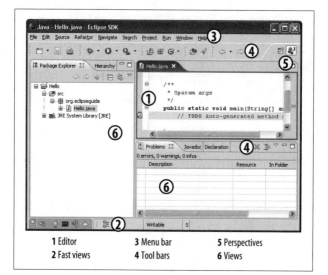

| 1 Editor | 3 Menu bar | 5 Perspectives |
| 2 Fast views | 4 Tool bars | 6 Views |

Figure 2. The Eclipse workbench is made up of views, editors, and other elements.

Views

A *view* is a window that lets you examine something, such as a list of files in your project. Eclipse comes with dozens of different views; see Table 2 for a partial list. These views are covered in more detail in Part VII.

Table 2. Commonly used Eclipse views

View name	Description
Package Explorer	Shows all your projects, Java packages, and files.
Hierarchy	Displays the class and interface relationships for the selected object.
Outline	Displays the structure of the currently open file.
Problems	Shows compiler errors and warnings in your code.
Console	Displays the output of your program.
Javadoc	Shows the description (from comments) of the selected object.
Declaration	Shows the source code where the selected object is declared.

To open a view, select Window → Show View. The most commonly used views are listed in that menu. To see the full list, select Other....

Most views have a titlebar that includes the icon and name for the view, a close icon, a toolbar, and an area for the content (see Figure 3 for an example showing the Outline view). Note that if the view is too narrow, the toolbar will be pushed to the next line. To discover what all the buttons do, move your mouse over a button, and a little window called a *tool tip* will appear that describes the item.

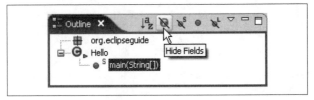

Figure 3. Views usually have titles, toolbars, and a content area. Let the mouse pointer hover over an item to bring up a description.

Multiple views can be stacked together in the same rectangular area. The titlebar will show a tab for each view, but only one view can be active at a time. Click on a tab to bring its view to the front. If the window is too narrow to show all the titles, a *chevron menu* will appear (see Figure 4; the number below the >> shows how many views are hidden). Click on the chevron menu to list the hidden views.

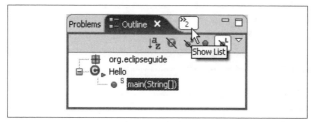

Figure 4. Views can be stacked on top of one another. If space is short, some may be hidden in a chevron menu.

Editors

An *editor* in Eclipse is just like any other editor—it lets you modify and save files. What sets editors in Eclipse apart is their built-in language-specific knowledge. In particular, the Java editor completely understands Java syntax; as you type, the editor can provide assistance such as underlining syntax errors and suggesting valid method and variable names (see Figure 5). Most of your time will be spent in the Java editor, but there are also editors for text, properties, and other types of files.

Editors share many characteristics with views. But unlike views, editors don't have toolbars, and you will usually have more than one of the same type of editor open (for example, several Java editors). Also, you can save or revert an editor's contents, but not a view's. An asterisk in the editor's titlebar indicates that the editor has unsaved data. Select File → Save or press Ctrl+S to write your changes to disk.

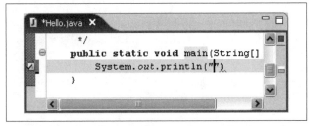

Figure 5. The Java editor provides typing assistance and immediate error detection.

Menus

Eclipse is filled with menus, yet it's not always obvious how to access them. So, let's take a quick tour. The most prominent one is the *main menu* across the top of the Eclipse window. Click on a menu item to activate it or press Alt and the shortcut key for the menu (for example Alt+F for the File menu).

Some views have *view menus* that open when you click on the downward-pointing triangle icon near the upper right of the view (see Figure 6 for an example).

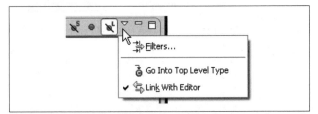

Figure 6. If you see a triangle in the toolbar, click on it for more options.

Another menu is hidden in the titlebar under the icon to the left of the title. Right-click on the icon to access the *system menu*; this allows you to close the view or editor, move it around, and so forth. The system menu is shown in Figure 7.

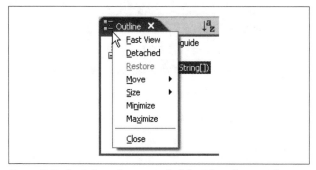

Figure 7. Right-click on the icon to the left of the title to get the system menu.

TIP

Most commands in Eclipse can be performed in several different ways. For example, to close a view you can either use the system menu or click on the close icon. Use whichever way is most convenient for you.

Finally, you can right-click on any item in the content area to bring up the *context menu* (see Figure 8). Notice the keyboard shortcuts listed to the right of the menu description. These shortcuts can be used instead of the menu to execute a particular command. For example, instead of right-clicking on main and selecting Open Type Hierarchy, you can just select main and press the F4 key.

TIP

Starting in Eclipse 3.1, you can press Ctrl+Shift+L to see a list of the current key definitions. To change them, go to Window → Preferences → General → Keys. By using key definitions and shortcuts, you can work in Eclipse without touching the mouse at all.

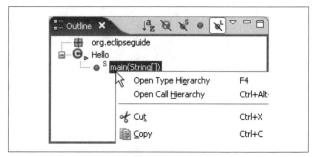

Figure 8. Right-click in the content area for the context menu.

Toolbars and Coolbars

A *toolbar* is a set of buttons (and sometimes other controls) that perform commonly used actions when you click on them. Usually toolbars appear near the top of the window that contains them. A collection of toolbars is called a *coolbar* (see Figure 9).

Figure 9. A coolbar is made up of toolbars. You reorder the individual toolbars by clicking and dragging the separators between them.

TIP

Most Eclipse documentation uses the term *toolbar* to refer to both toolbars and coolbars, so the rest of this book will do the same unless it's necessary to make a special distinction between the two.

In the "Views" section, you saw some examples of toolbars that were part of views. The toolbar at the top of the Workbench window is called the *main toolbar* (seen back in

Figure 2). As you edit different files, the main toolbar will change to show tools that apply to the current editor.

Perspectives

A *perspective* is a set of views, editors, and toolbars, along with their arrangement on your desktop. Think of a perspective as a way of looking at your work that is optimized for a specific kind of task, such as writing programs.

As you perform a task, you may rearrange windows, open new views, and so on. Your arrangement is saved under the current perspective. The next time you have to perform the same kind of task, simply switch to that perspective, and Eclipse will put everything back the way you left it.

To switch perspectives, select Window → Open Perspective or click on the Open Perspective icon (to the right of the main toolbar). This will bring up a list of the most commonly used perspectives; select Other... to see the full list.

Eclipse comes with several perspectives already defined; these are shown in Table 3.

Table 3. Built-in Eclipse perspectives

Perspective	Purpose
Resource	Arrange your files and projects.
Java	Develop programs in the Java language.
Debug	Diagnose and debug problems that occur at runtime.
Java Browsing	Explore your code in a Smalltalk-like environment.
Java Type Hierarchy	Explore your code based on class relationships.
Plug-in Development	Create add-ins to Eclipse.
CVS Repository Exploring	Browse a source code repository, including its files and revision history.
Team Synchronizing	Merge changes you've made with those of your teammates.

Each perspective has a set of views associated with it that are open by default. For example, the Java perspective starts with the Package Explorer view open. If you don't like the default, close any views you don't want and open others with Window → Show View.

TIP

Sometimes Eclipse will offer to switch perspectives for you. For example, if you're in the Resource perspective and create a Java project, it will ask if you'd like to switch to the Java perspective. Usually the best thing is to answer Yes and have it remember your decision so it won't ask you again.

Perspectives are there for your convenience. Feel free to customize them all you want. To restore a perspective to its factory default, select Window → Reset Perspective. To save your perspective under a different name, select Window → Save Perspective As…. The new perspective will show up in the Window → Open Perspective → Other… menu.

Rearranging Views and Editors

Views and editors can be shown side by side or stacked on top of other views and editors. To move a view or editor, simply click on its titlebar and drag it to a new location (see Figure 10). The only restrictions are that editors have to stay in their own rectangular area, and they can't be mixed with views. However, you can arrange the views around the editors, and you can even drag views outside of the main Eclipse window (these are called *tear-off views*). You can also collapse a view to an icon on the edge of the window (this is called a *fast view*).

Pay close attention to the changing cursor as you drag a window; the cursor shape indicates where the window will end up when you let go of the mouse button. Table 4 shows the cursor shapes and what they mean.

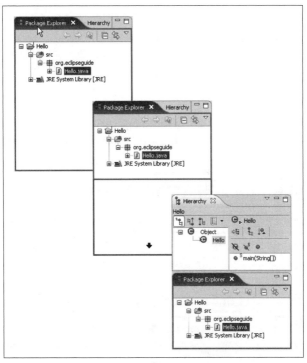

Figure 10. You can see how the Package Explorer is dragged from a tab into the bottom of the window.

Table 4. Cursor shapes while dragging views and editors

Cursor shape	Final position of the view/editor being dragged
⬆	Above the window under the cursor
⬇	Below the window under the cursor
⬅	To the left of the window under the cursor
➡	To the right of the window under the cursor
🗗	On top of a stack of windows under the cursor
◀	In the fast view area (it will slide out as needed or when manually clicked)
⊞	Outside the main window

To change the relative size of side-by-side views or editors,
move the mouse cursor to the thin dividing line between two
of them. The cursor shape will change, indicating you can
move that divider by clicking it and dragging it to the desired
location.

Maximizing and Minimizing

Sometimes you need to focus temporarily on a single view or
editor. For example, you might want to hide all the views
and use the whole Eclipse window to look at one large file in
the editor. You could resize the editor manually by dragging
its edges, but an easier way is to *maximize* the editor.

Double-click on the view or editor's titlebar (or click on the
maximize icon) to make it expand; double-click again (or use
the restore icon) to restore the window to its original size.
When a window is maximized, you won't be able to see any
of the other views or editors outside of the current stack.

As an alternative, you can temporarily shrink the other stacks
of windows by clicking on the *minimize* icon (next to the
maximize icon at the top of the view or editor). This hides
the content area, showing only the titlebar. It works best on
horizontal views and editors.

Remember, you can save your favorite window arrangements as named perspectives.

You could spend hours exploring all the options to customize your Eclipse workbench, but that's not what you're here for, right? Part III will get you started with Java development in Eclipse.

Java Done Quick

Get your stopwatch ready because we're going to create and run some simple Java code as quickly as possible. Ready... set...go!

Creating a Project

An Eclipse *project* is just a directory that holds your program's resources (source code, icons, and so forth). Usually projects are subdirectories in your workspace (see the "Specify a Workspace" section in Part I). You can import an existing project, but for this exercise, we'll make one from scratch.

To create a project, select File → New → Project... and then double-click Java Project. This opens the New Java Project wizard (see Figure 11).

For "Project name," type in something original like **Hello**. Under "Project layout," enable the "Create separate source and output folders" option.

TIP

As a best practice, always use separate directories for the source and output folders.

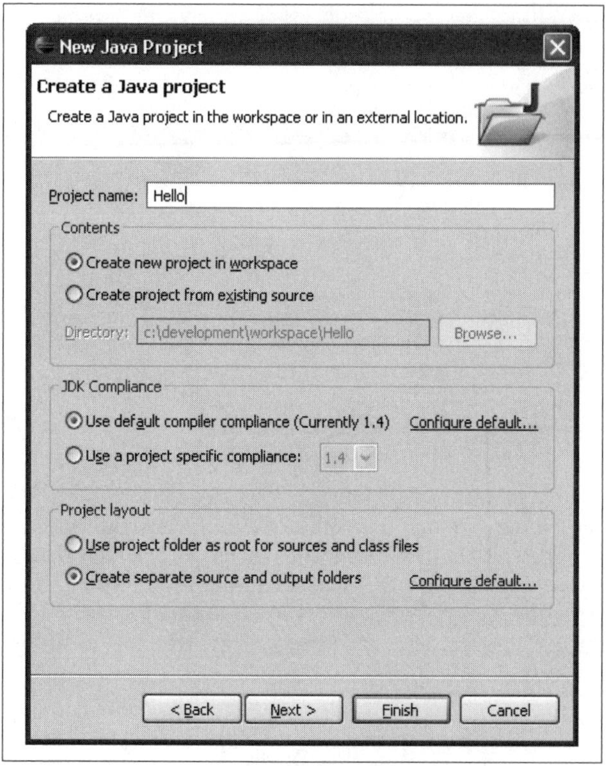

Figure 11. The New Java Project wizard configures a new directory for your code.

Click Finish to accept the default options and let Eclipse create the project. If you see a dialog that says Confirm Perspective Switch, enable the "Remember my decision" option and click Yes. Also, if you see a dialog about Java 5.0 compliance, enable compliance for the entire workspace (not just the project).

After a moment, you should see your new empty project in the Package Explorer view (see Figure 12).

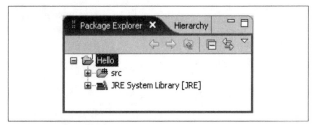

Figure 12. A new Java project is born.

Creating a Package

A Java *package* is a standard way to organize your classes into separate namespaces. Although you can create classes without packages, doing so is considered bad programming practice. To create a new package, select File → New → Package or click on the New Package icon in the main toolbar (🏴). Enter the package name as **org.eclipseguide** and click Finish. You can see the results in the Package Explorer, as shown in Figure 13.

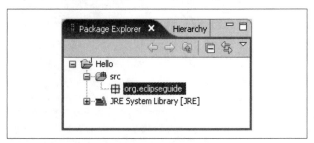

Figure 13. The project has grown a package.

Creating a Class

With the org.eclipseguide package highlighted, select File → New → Class or click on the New Java Class icon (🞇). Enter the name of the class, starting with a capital letter. For this example, enter **Hello**.

Under the section of the dialog that asks which method stubs you would like to create, select the option to create public static void main(String[] args).

Leave the rest of the options set to their default values and click Finish. Eclipse will generate the code for the class for you (this generated class is shown in Figure 14), and open the Java editor with your new class in view.

Entering Code

You could run the program now, but it wouldn't be very interesting. So, let's add a few lines to print something out. Start by deleting the generated comment that says:

```
// TODO Auto-generated method stub
```

Figure 14. Now the package has a file in it. You can further expand the file to see its classes.

Then replace it with this code:

```
for (int i = 0; i < 10; i++) {
    System.out.println(
        "Hello, world " + i);
}
```

When you're done, the Java editor should look similar to Figure 15.

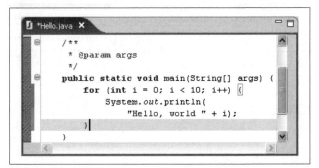

Figure 15. This is 10 times better than the usual "Hello, world" program.

The editor looks innocent enough, but through its clever use of colors and annotations, the window is quietly conveying a great deal of information. A large number of options to control this information can be found under Window → Preferences → Java → Editor.

TIP

Press Ctrl+Shift+F (or select Source → Format) to reformat your code and fix any indentation and spacing problems. Do this early and often. If you'd like, you can customize the formatting rules in the Java preferences.

Running the Program

Press Ctrl+S (or select File → Save) to write the code to disk and compile it. In the Package Explorer, right-click on *Hello.java* and select Run As → Java Application. The program will run, and the Console view will open to show the output (see Figure 16).

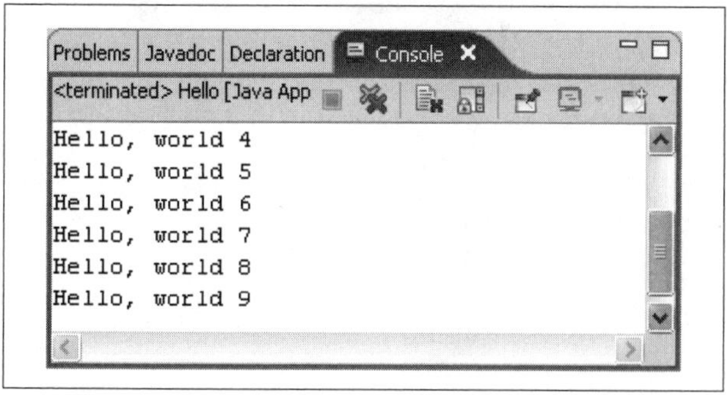

Figure 16. Isn't this exciting?

That's it! You've written, compiled, and run your first program in Eclipse in just a few minutes. Now, try it again and see if you can do it in under a minute. My record is 35 seconds. Go ahead, I'll wait.

TIP

After you have run the program once, you can press Ctrl+F11 (Run → Run Last Launched) or click on the Run icon in the toolbar () to run it again.

Now that you're ready to write the next killer app, what's the rest of the book for? Part IV will introduce you to your new best pal, the Java debugger. If your programs never have any bugs (ahem), you can skip ahead to Part V to learn about unit testing or Part VI to pick up a few tips about using the IDE.

Debugging

Let's face it: all but the most trivial programs have bugs in them. Eclipse provides a powerful debugger to help you find and eliminate those bugs quickly. This part of the book will give you a head start in understanding how to use the Eclipse debugger.

Running the Debugger

Running your program under the control of the debugger is similar to running it normally. Right-click on the file containing your main method (*Hello.java*) and select Debug As → Java Application. Or, if you have run or debugged the program before, just press F11 (or select Run → Debug Last Launched), or click on the Debug button (🐞) in the main toolbar.

Go ahead and try that now. What happened? The program ran to completion and sent its output to the Console view just as if you had run the class normally. You have to set a breakpoint to actually take advantage of the debugger.

Setting Breakpoints

A *breakpoint* is a marker you place on a line of code where you want the debugger to pause execution. To set one, double-click in the gutter area to the left of the source line. For this example, we want to stop on the System.out.println( ) call, so double-click in the gutter next to that line. A breakpoint indicator will appear, as shown in Figure 17.

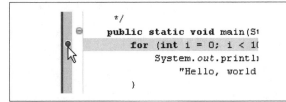

Figure 17. Set a breakpoint by double-clicking to the left of the source line.

Now, press F11 and Eclipse will run your program again in debug mode. The breakpoint indicator will change when the class is loaded, and the debugger will stop at the line where you added the breakpoint.

TIP

One of the nice things about breakpoints in Eclipse is that they stay with the line even if the line number changes (e.g., due to code being added or removed above it).

When the breakpoint is reached and the program stops, you'll notice several things. First, Eclipse will switch to the Debug perspective. If you see a dialog asking to confirm the perspective switch, select "Remember my decision" and click Yes.

TIP

Using one perspective for coding and another for debugging is optional, but some people like being able to customize their window arrangement for each task. You can disable this switching in the Run/Debug preferences (Window → Preferences → Run/Debug).

Next, several new views will open—most importantly, the Debug view (see Figure 18). This view lets you control all the threads of execution of all the programs being debugged. Finally, the line of code where you put the breakpoint will be highlighted to indicate which line will be executed next.

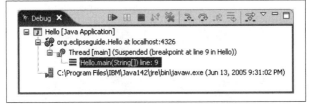

Figure 18. The Debug view lets you control and monitor execution of multiple programs and threads.

To continue running after a breakpoint, click on the Resume button in the Debug view's toolbar (▸) or press F8 (Run → Resume). Execution will continue until the next breakpoint is hit or the program terminates.

TIP

If your program is in a long-running loop, click on the Suspend button (▯▯) or select Run → Suspend to make it stop. Or, just add a new breakpoint at any time—the program does not have to be stopped.

You can see a list of all your breakpoints in the Breakpoints view. Here you can enable and disable breakpoints, make them conditional on certain program values, or set *exception breakpoints* (i.e., to stop when a Java exception is thrown).

Single Stepping

Like most debuggers, the one provided by the Eclipse IDE lets you step line by line through your program with one of two commands: *step into* (🐾; F5; or Run → Step Into) and *step over* (🐾; F6; or Run → Step Over). The difference between the two is apparent when the current line is a method call. If you step into the current line, the debugger will go to the first line of the method. If you step over the current line, the debugger will run the method and stop on the next line.

Try stepping now, by running until your breakpoint is hit and then pressing F6 several times in a row. Watch the highlight bar move around as the current line changes.

If you step into a method call and then change your mind, execute the *step return* command (🐾; F7; or Run → Step Return). This lets the program run until the current method returns. The debugger will stop at the line following the line that called the method.

Looking at Variables

The Eclipse IDE provides many different ways to examine and modify your program state. For example, as you single step, you may have noticed that the Variables window shows the current value of all the local variables, parameters, and fields that are currently visible (see Figure 19). You can quickly identify which variables are changing because Eclipse draws them in a different color. If any of the variables are nonprimitives (objects or arrays), you can expand them to look at the individual elements.

To change the value of a variable, first select it in the Variables view. This will make its current value appear in the bottom half of the window, where you can change it. Save the new value by pressing Ctrl+S (or right-click and select Assign Value).

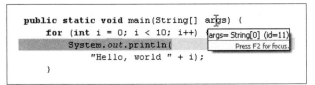

Figure 19. The Variables view shows all the values in scope. Changes since the last step or resume are highlighted in red.

TIP

When you are coding, try to use the smallest possible scope for your local variables. For example, instead of declaring all your variables at the top of a function, declare them inside the statement blocks (curly braces) where they are actually used. Besides being a good programming practice, this will limit the number of items displayed in the Variables view.

Another way to see the value of a particular variable is to move your cursor over it in the source editor. After a short pause, a tool tip window will appear with the value. See Figure 20 for an example.

```
public static void main(String[] args) {
    for (int i = 0; i < 10; i++) {args= String[0] (id=11)
        System.out.println(                     Press F2 for focus.
            "Hello, world " + i);
    }
```

Figure 20. Hover the mouse over a variable in the Java editor to see its current value.

What if you need to see the value of a Java expression? No problem: just use the mouse or keyboard to select the expression in the editor, then press Ctrl+Shift+D (or right-click and select Display). Eclipse will evaluate the expression (including any side effects) and show the results in a pop-up window (see Figure 21). The expression can be as simple or as complicated as you like, as long as it's valid.

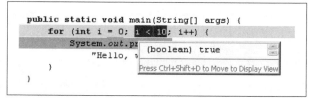

```
public static void main(String[] args) {
    for (int i = 0; i < 10; i++) {
        System.out.pr
            "Hello, 
    }
}
```
(boolean) true
Press Ctrl+Shift+D to Move to Display View

Figure 21. Select an expression and press Ctrl+Shift+D to evaluate it.

For compound objects like class instances, you may want to try the Inspect command (Ctrl+Shift+I, or right-click and select Inspect) instead of Display. This will let you expand items and collapse members as in the Variables view.

Changing Code on the Fly

Eclipse blurs the line between editing and debugging by letting you modify a running program. You don't have to stop the program—just edit and save it. If possible, Eclipse will compile just the class that was modified and insert it into the running process. This handy feature is called *hot code replace*.

TIP

If you modify a method that the program is currently executing, the debugger will have to drop to the previous frame and begin that method again from its first line. This doesn't work on the main( ) method because there is no caller.

Some kinds of changes can be made on the fly and some cannot. Simple things (like fixing an expression formula, changing comments, adding new local variables, adding new statements to an existing method, etc.) should work fine. If for some reason execution cannot continue, you will get an error dialog with the option to continue without making the change, terminate the program, or terminate and restart it from the beginning.

TIP

Hot code replace requires special support from the Java virtual machine that is not present in all versions of Java. It's known to work in Sun's Java Version 1.4.2 and later, but not all vendors support it. If your Java version does not support it, you'll get an error dialog when you try to save.

The debugger has so many features that it's impossible to cover them all here. Part VI covers more advanced topics that impact running and debugging your program, especially in the "Launch Configurations" section. But in your first pass through this book, you may want to continue with Part V, which covers unit testing. Later, you can go to Part VII to find out what all those buttons in the Debug and Breakpoint views do.

The Eclipse online help is also a good resource for information on running and debugging. See the following sections in the User's Guide (Help → Help Contents → Java Development User Guide):

- Concepts → Debugger
- Tasks → Running and debugging

Unit Testing with JUnit

JUnit is a regression testing framework written by Kent Beck and Erich Gamma. Since Erich is the project leader for Eclipse's Java toolkit, it's only natural that JUnit is well integrated into the IDE.

A Simple Factorial Demo

To try out unit testing in Eclipse, first create a project called *Factorial* containing a class called Factorial. Inside that class, create a factorial( ) method as follows:

```java
public class Factorial {
    public static double factorial(int x) {
        if (x == 0)
            return 1.0;
        return x + factorial(x - 1);
    }
}
```

TIP

If you notice the nasty little error in this code, ignore it for now. That's part of the demonstration!

Creating Test Cases

To test this class, you'll need to create a test case for it. A *test case* is a class that extends the JUnit TestCase class and contains test methods that exercise your code. To create a test case, right-click on *Factorial.java* in the Package Explorer and select New → JUnit Test Case.

TIP

If you get a dialog offering to add the JUnit library to the build path, select Yes.

A dialog window will come up with the name of the test case (FactorialTest) already filled in, along with the name of the class being tested. Click Next to show the Test Methods dialog, select the factorial(int) method, and click Finish to generate the test case. Eclipse will then generate some code for you, similar to the following:

```java
public class FactorialTest extends TestCase {
    public void testFactorial() {
    }
}
```

Now, all you need to do is supply the contents of the testFactorial() method. JUnit provides a number of static methods that you call in your tests to make assertions about your program's behavior. See Table 5 for a list.

Table 5. JUnit assertion methods

Method	Description
assertEquals() assertNotEquals()	See if two objects or primitives have the same value.
assertSame() assertNotSame()	See if two objects are the same object.
assertTrue() assertFalse()	Test a Boolean expression.
assertNull() assertNotNull()	Test for a null object.

To test the factorial( ) method, call the method with a few sample values and make sure it returns the right results. Now, insert a blank line and press Ctrl+Space (this brings up the *code assist* feature, which is discussed in Part VI); you will discover that JUnit supplies a version of assertEquals( ) that takes three arguments. The first two are the values to compare, the last is a "fuzz factor;" assertEquals( ) will fail if the difference between the supplied values is greater than the fuzz factor. Supply the value you expect the method to return as the first parameter; use the method call itself as the second. For example,

```java
public void testFactorial( ) {
    assertEquals(1.0,
        Factorial.factorial(0), 0.0);
    assertEquals(1.0,
        Factorial.factorial(1), 0.0);
    assertEquals(120.0,
        Factorial.factorial(5), 0.0);
}
```

Feel free to insert a few more assertions in this method or add additional test methods.

You can also override the setUp( ) and tearDown( ) methods, respectively, to create and destroy any resources needed by each test, such as a network connection or file handle.

TIP

All test methods must start with the word "test" so JUnit can figure out which methods to run. JUnit will ignore any methods in the test class that it doesn't recognize.

Running Tests

To run the test case, right-click on *FactorialTest.java* and select Run As → JUnit Test. The JUnit view appears, and your tests are off and running. In this case, a red progress bar and a special icon next to the view title indicate that something went wrong (see Figure 22).

Figure 22. The JUnit view shows a summary of the last test run.

If you double-click on the test class or method name in the Failures list, Eclipse will open that test in the editor. Double-click on a line in the Failure Trace to go to a specific line number.

TIP

The best practice if a test fails is to set a breakpoint on the failing line and then use the debugger to diagnose the problem. Just select Debug instead of Run to run the debugger.

When you examine the test, you can see that the factorial function is not being calculated correctly, due to an error in the formula. To correct the error, replace the + with a *:

```
return x * factorial(x - 1);
```

Now, rerun your tests (Ctrl+F11). You shouldn't see any failures; instead, you should see a green bar, indicating success.

Test First

Having a good suite of tests is important—so important, that many developers advocate writing the tests for new code before a single line of the code itself! This is called *test driven development*, or TDD for short. Such tests represent the requirements that your code must satisfy in order to be considered correct.

To see how Eclipse makes TDD simple, keep the unit test you just created, but delete the *Factorial.java* file (select it in the Package Explorer and press Delete). The editor for the FactorialTest class will shown an error immediately because the Factorial class is not defined anymore. This simulates the state you would be in if you had written your test class first.

Put the text cursor on the first line that has an error and press Ctrl+1 (Edit → Quick Fix). Select the "Create class 'Factorial'" option and press Enter. When the New Java Class dialog appears, press Enter to accept the defaults.

Now, go back to the FactorialTest editor and note that the compiler complains that there is no factorial(int) method. Press Ctrl+1 to create one.

Unfortunately, the current version of Eclipse is not always smart enough to figure out the right return type, so you may need to change the generated return type to be a double. Use a dummy return value (0.0) for now. At this point, *Factorial.java* should look something like this:

```java
public static double factorial(int i) {
    return 0.0;
}
```

Now you have a test case, a little bit of code, and no errors—so try running the tests. Unsurprisingly, they fail. At this point in actual TDD, you would go back to the code being tested and fix it so that it passes the tests, then add another test, make that work, and repeat the process until done.

Compare this technique with what most people typically do. They write a bunch of code first, then write a trivial little test program to exercise that code (maybe something with a main( ) method and a few println( ) statements). Once that test is working, they throw the test away and assume their class will never break again.

Don't ever throw tests away! Nurture them, slowly add to them, and run them often, preferably as part of an automated build and test system. Techniques even exist to create unit tests for user interfaces.

The JUnit view is covered in more detail in Part VII. If you want to learn more about unit testing best practices, see:

http://www.junit.org
    JUnit home page

http://www.testdriven.com
    Resource for test driven development

PART VI

Tips and Tricks

The Eclipse IDE has an incredibly rich set of features, but many of them are hidden from view. With a little digging, you can discover its secrets and get the most out of the environment. This part of the book gets you started with several useful but less visible features.

Code Assist

The Java editor is always paying attention to what you type, ready to offer helpful suggestions through a feature called *code assist* (also called *content assist*). To use it, go to the Java editor in the Hello example and start a new statement in the main( ) method. Begin typing the following:

```
System.
```

Pause after the period. A code assist window (similar to that shown in Figure 23) will appear. The window shows you all the valid possibilities at this point. Type the letter **o** and the choices will narrow down to out. Press Enter to accept this choice. Given the long names most Java programs use, this can be a real time-saver.

Besides reducing typing, code assist is especially handy when you are exploring unfamiliar territory—for example, making calls to a library you haven't used before. Code assist is activated automatically by certain keystrokes—like the period in the previous example—but you can also invoke it at any time by pressing Ctrl+Space (Edit → Content Assist). This feature

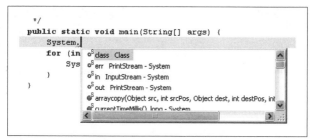

Figure 23. Code assist tells you what comes next and displays any Javadoc (if the source is available).

is fully configurable in the Java editor preferences (Window → Preferences → Java → Editor).

Templates

Eclipse provides a shorthand way of entering text called *templates*. For example, in the Java editor, if you type **for** and press Ctrl+Space, the code assist window will pop up as before, but this time it will display a few templates that start with the word "for" (see Figure 24).

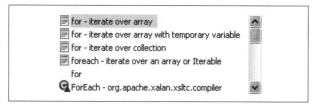

Figure 24. Editor templates are shorthand for entering boilerplate text (e.g., for loops).

Selecting the first one will cause code similar to this to appear in the editor:

```java
for (int i = 0; i < array.length; i++) {

}
```

The cursor highlights the first variable i. If you start typing, all three occurrences of that variable will be modified. Pressing Tab will cause the variable array to be selected; pressing Tab again will put the cursor on the blank line between the braces so you can supply the body of the loop.

TIP

If you try this, you may see different variable names. Eclipse guesses which variables to use based on the surrounding code.

For a list of all predefined templates, and to create your own or export them to an XML file, see Window → Preferences → Java → Editor → Templates.

Automatic Typing

Closely related to code assist is a feature called *automatic typing*. If you're following along with the earlier example shown in Figure 23, the text cursor should be positioned after System.out. Type **.println(** (that is, period, **println**, opening parenthesis). The Java editor will type the closing parenthesis for you automatically. Now, type a double quote, and the closing quote appears. Type in some text and then press the Tab key. Tab advances to the next valid place for input, which is after the closing quote. Hit Tab again, and the cursor advances to the end. Type a semicolon to finish the statement.

TIP

Code assist and automatic typing take a little getting used to. At first you may be tempted to turn them off, but I suggest you give it time and try to learn to work with them. After a while, you'll wonder how you ever got by without the extra support.

Refactoring

Refactoring means transforming code without changing its functionality. Consider renaming, which is the simplest form of refactoring. If you rename a local variable from rose to daisy, it would smell as sweet.

Much has been written on refactoring, such as *Refactoring: Improving the Design of Existing Code* (Addison Wesley). Before Eclipse and similar tools were available, programmers had to do refactoring manually or with simple text substitutions. For example, in the *vi* editor, running the command :1,$s/rose/daisy/g will replace "rose" with "daisy" everywhere in the current file.

If you've ever tried this, you know it's usually a bad idea. Your simple search-and-replace operation can change more than just the variable you intended, even with a clever substitution string. Plus, if you need to change multiple files, you'll have to go to a scripting language such as Perl.

Here's how it works in Eclipse. To rename a symbol (i.e., a class, method, variable, etc.), select it in the editor and press Alt+Shift+R (Refactor → Rename). Type in the new name and press Enter to perform the change. Done!

If you like, you can select the Preview button before performing the changes; this will show you what the modified source will look like (see Figure 25). You can also undo the refactoring (Ctrl+Z or Edit → Undo) if you change your mind.

Here's another handy refactoring supported by Eclipse: to move a class from one package to another, simply go to the Package Explorer view and drag the file to where you want it. Eclipse will take care of changing the package statement in the file and in all the other class files that refer to it. Neat, huh?

Eclipse implements over a dozen different types of refactorings, and more are being added all the time. See the Java Development User Guide (Window → Help Contents → Java

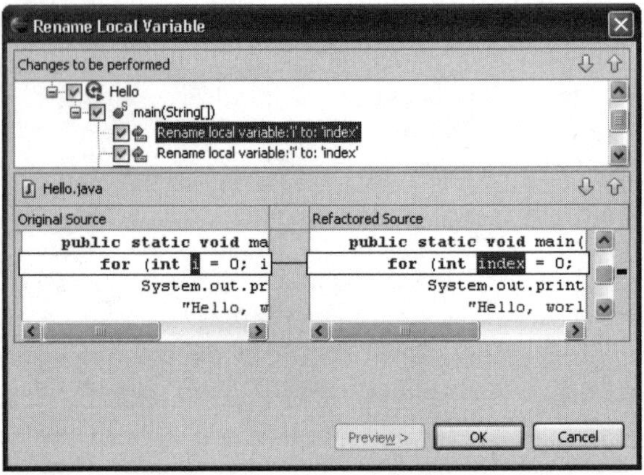

Figure 25. You can preview the changes that any of Eclipse's refactorings would make.

Development User Guide) under Reference → Refactoring for more information.

Hover Help

You've seen that code assist is a good way to explore an unfamiliar API. Another useful tool is *hover help*. To use hover help, simply move the mouse cursor over a symbol you want to know more about and pause for a moment. For example, try hovering over println in System.out.println. A little pop-up window will appear, giving you a short description of the method.

For best results, you need access to the source code of the symbol you are examining. For Java library methods, the source comes with the JDK (J2SE SDK) package. Eclipse can usually figure out how to find this source code on its own, but see Window → Preferences → Java → Installed JREs to configure the JDK's location.

If you are using code from a third-party JAR file, the source is often provided in a separate file or a subdirectory. You can tell Eclipse about this location by right-clicking on the JAR file in the Package Explorer and selecting Properties → Java Source Attachment.

If you don't have the source code, but you have the API documentation (Javadoc) in HTML form, select the symbol you want information on and press Shift+F2 (Navigate → Open External Javadoc). To make this work, you have to configure the Javadoc URL in the properties for the JAR file: right-click on the JAR file and select Properties → Javadoc Location.

Hyperlinks

Did you know there is a web browser built into the Java editor? Well, there is—sort of. The editor lets you navigate around your program as if it were a web site. Hold down the Ctrl key and move your mouse through your source code. An underline will appear to indicate hyperlinked symbols. You can leave the mouse cursor over the symbol to see its definition, or click on it to open the declaration in the editor.

Like a browser, Eclipse maintains a history of all the pages you've visited. Use the Back command (⇦; Alt+Left; or Navigate → Left) to go to the previous location, and use Forward (⇨; Alt+Right; or Navigate → Right) to go to the next one.

Quick Fixes

Whenever you make a syntax error in your program, Eclipse's background compiler detects it immediately and draws an error indicator (affectionately known as the *red squiggle*) under the offending code. In addition to simply detecting the problem, Eclipse can usually offer an automatic program correction, called a *quick fix*.

For example, try misspelling the System.out method println as **printline**. Press Ctrl+1 (Edit → Quick Fix) to see several possible fixes. One of them will be Change to println(..). Press the down arrow to see a preview of each proposed change; press Enter to accept the one you want.

The Quick Fix command can also make suggestions for small source transformations on lines that don't have errors. For example, if you have code like this:

```
if (!(hail || thunder))
```

and you select the text (!(hail || thunder) and press Ctrl+1, Eclipse will suggest some possible transformations, such as "Push negation down." Choosing that particular option would change the code to:

```
if (!hail && !thunder)
```

Searching

The Eclipse IDE provides dozens of different ways to locate things. Eclipse breaks these up into two major categories:

Find
    Look for something in the current file.

Search
    Look for something in multiple files.

The Find command (Ctrl+F or Edit → Find/Replace) is just a run-of-the-mill text locator like you would see in any editor. You can look for plain strings or full regular expressions, and you can optionally substitute the text you find with other text. The shortcut to find the next occurrence is Ctrl+K.

A handy variant on Find is *incremental find*, a feature borrowed from the Emacs editor. Press Ctrl+J (Edit → Incremental Find Next) and start typing the text you're looking for. The selection will move to the next occurrence as you type.

Searches are much more interesting. To start with, Eclipse supports locating strings and regular expressions in many files at once. You can search the entire workspace, just the current project, or any subset (called a *working set*) that you define. To do this kind of search, select Search → File....

Eclipse can also do a full language-aware search. Since Eclipse has its own built-in Java compiler, it understands the difference between, say, a method named fact and a field named fact, or even between two methods that have the same names but take different parameters, such as fact(int) and fact(double). This kind of search is available by selecting Search → Java....

These searches and more are accessible through the Search dialog (🔍; Ctrl+H; or Search → Search). The most common variations also have direct menus or shortcuts of their own. For example, to find all references to a symbol, select the symbol and press Ctrl+Shift+G (or Search → References → Workspace). To find the symbol's declaration, press Ctrl+G (Search → Declarations → Workspace). To find only those places where the symbol is modified, try Search → Write Access → Workspace.

TIP

Current versions of Eclipse don't allow you to perform searches on arbitrary files in the filesystem, but you can use an advanced option under File → New → Folder to link outside directories into your workspace and then search them.

All search results will appear, naturally enough, in the Search view. See Part VII for more details on that view.

Scrapbook Pages

A *scrapbook page* is a way to create and test snippets of code without all the trappings of normal Java code. In some ways, it's like working in a scripting language, but you have the full expressiveness of Java in addition to being able to make calls into any of your code or any of the system libraries.

To create a scrapbook page, select File → New → Other… → Java → Java Run/Debug → Scrapbook Page. Enter the name of the page—for example, **test**—and click Finish (or just press Enter). A new editor page will open for *test.jpage*.

In the blank scrapbook page, try typing in an expression like **123/456**, press Ctrl+A to select the expression, and press Ctrl+Shift+D (Run → Display) to run it and display the result. (The answer in this case is (int) 0 because both numbers are integers and the result was truncated.) Note that the result is selected, so you can copy it quickly (or press Backspace to remove it from the page).

Next, try entering **Math.PI** and displaying its result. This works because the scrapbook page already has all the system libraries imported, including the Math class. If you need a particular import, you can bring up the context menu and select Set Imports….

Let's try something a little more complicated. Type in this snippet of code:

```
double d = 3.14;
System.out.println(d);
```

Now select the snippet and press Ctrl+U (Run → Execute) to execute it. The output will appear in the Console window. Execute is exactly like Display except that Execute doesn't show the return value (if any).

You can execute loops or even call methods in your regular programs from the scrapbook page. This is useful for trying out new ideas or just for simple debugging.

Java Build Path

If you've done any Java programming before, you're familiar with the Java classpath—a list of directories and JAR files containing Java classes that make up the program. Usually this is controlled by an environment variable (CLASSPATH) or a command-line option (-cp).

In Eclipse, classpath details are a little more complicated. The first thing to realize is that Eclipse doesn't use the CLASSPATH environment variable. It understands and controls the location of all classes itself. Additionally, Eclipse makes a distinction between runtime and build (compile) time. In Eclipse terminology, *classpath* refers only to the runtime class list, while *build path* refers to the compile-time list. These two paths may be different, but, by default, they will both be set to the list you specify in the build path.

To see the build path, right-click on your project and select Properties → Java Build Path. A dialog will appear, with the tabs described in Table 6.

Table 6. Java Build Path tabs

Tab name	Description
Source	Tell the Java compiler where your source code is located. Each source directory is the root of a package tree. You can also control where generated output files (such as *.class* files) go.
Projects	Make the current project depend on other projects. Classes in the other projects will be recognized at build time and runtime. The other projects do not have to be built into a JAR file before referring to them in Eclipse; this cuts down on development time.
Libraries	Pull in code that is not in Eclipse projects, such as JAR files. See Table 7 for the kinds of locations you can access.
Order and Export	If other projects are dependent on this one, expose (or don't expose) symbols in the current project to the other projects.

In addition to going through the Java Build Path dialog, you can right-click on directories and JAR files in the Package

Explorer view and select commands under the Build Path menu to add and remove items from the build path.

The Libraries tab is very flexible about the locations it allows you to specify for JARs and class files. Other features in Eclipse use similar lists, so if you understand this tab, it will help you understand those features as well. Table 7 explains the buttons on the Libraries tab.

Table 7. JAR and class locations in the Java Build Path

Button name	Description
Add JARs…	Specify JAR files in the workspace (this project or other projects).
Add External JARs…	Specify full pathnames for JAR files outside the workspace (not recommended for team projects).
Add Variable…	Use a symbolic variable name (like `JRE_LIB` or `ECLIPSE_HOME`) to refer to a JAR file outside the workspace.
Add Library…	Refer to a directory outside the workspace containing several JAR files.
Add Class Folder…	Refer to a workspace directory containing individual class files.

Launch Configurations

How do you specify command-line parameters to your program or change the Java VM options that are used to invoke your program? Every time you select Run As → Java Application on a new class that has a main( ) method, Eclipse creates a launch configuration for you. A *launch configuration* is the set of all the options used to run your program.

To change those options, select Run → Run… and locate your configuration in the dialog. Click on the configuration to see all the options in a series of tabbed pages on the right-hand side of the window (the tabs are described in Table 8). You can also create new configurations in this dialog.

Table 8. Launch configuration tabs

Tab name	Description
Main	Specify the project and the name of the Main class.
Arguments	Set the program arguments, the Java VM arguments, and the working directory in which to start the program.
JRE	Specify the version of Java used to run the program (this can be different than the one used to compile it).
Classpath	Set the list of JARs and classes available at runtime.
Source	Locate the source code inside or outside the workspace.
Environment	Pass environment variables to the program.
Common	Miscellaneous options.

Many more features of Eclipse are waiting to be discovered, and new ones are added in each release. The "Tips and Tricks" section of the online help (Help → Tips and Tricks) is a good place to look for the kinds of little nuggets that can save you time or let you do something new. You can also find a useful command and keyboard shortcut listing in the Appendix.

PART VII

Views

Eclipse has so many different views and toolbars that it's easy to get overwhelmed trying to decipher them all. Consider this part of the book to be your own personal secret decoder ring.

Breakpoints View

The Breakpoints view (in the Debug perspective) shows a list of all the breakpoints you have set in your projects. Use it to enable and disable breakpoints, edit their properties, and set *exception breakpoints* (which trigger a stop when a Java exception occurs). Table 9 lists the commands on the Breakpoints view toolbar.

Table 9. Breakpoints view toolbar

Icon	Description
	Remove the selected breakpoint(s).
	Remove all breakpoints in all projects.
	Show/hide breakpoints not valid in the selected remote debug target (toggle).
	Edit the source code at the breakpoint.
	Temporarily disable all breakpoints (toggle).
	Expand the breakpoint tree.

Table 9. Breakpoints view toolbar (continued)

Icon	Description
	Collapse the breakpoint tree.
	When the program stops, highlight the breakpoint that caused it to stop (toggle).
	Create a breakpoint for a Java exception.

Double-click on a breakpoint to edit the code at that line. To fine-tune when the breakpoint will be triggered, right-click on the breakpoint and select Properties. Table 10 shows some of the properties you can set. The exact options that appear will vary depending on the breakpoint's type.

Table 10. Breakpoint properties

Property	Description
Enabled	Indicates whether the breakpoint is currently in effect.
Hit Count	Specifies how many times the breakpoint must be hit before the programs stops.
Condition	Stops only when the expression is true or changes value.
Suspend Policy	Pauses the whole program or just a single thread.
Filtering	Limits the breakpoint's effect to the given thread(s).

In the Eclipse Java development environment, an *expression* is anything you can put on the righthand side of a Java assignment statement. This can include ordinary variables, fields, method calls, arithmetic formulae, and so forth.

A *conditional breakpoint* is a breakpoint that doesn't stop every time. For example, if you're debugging a crash that occurs on the 100th time through a loop, you could put a breakpoint at the top of the loop and use a conditional expression like i == 99, or you could specify a hit count of 100—whichever is more convenient.

Console View

The Console view displays the output of programs that are run under the control of Eclipse. Use it to view standard output or error output from your Java programs, or from Ant, CVS, or any other external program launched from Eclipse. You can also type into the Console view to provide standard input.

The Console view is closely tied to the Debug view. It keeps a separate page for each program listed in the Debug view, whether or not the program is currently running. Table 11 shows the commands on the Console view's toolbar.

Table 11. Console view toolbar

Icon	Description
▣	Terminate the current program.
✖	Remove all record of previously terminated programs.
▣	Clear all the lines in the current console page.
▣	Keep the view from scrolling as new lines are added to the end (toggle).
☑	Prevent the view from automatically switching to other pages (toggle).
▣	Switch to an existing console page.
☑	Open a new console page (for example, to see CVS output).

TIP

If your program prints a stack traceback, the Console view turns each line into a hyperlink. Click on a link to go to the location indicated in the traceback.

Options for the Console view can be found under Window → Preferences → Run/Debug → Console.

Debug View

The Debug view (in the Debug perspective) lists all programs that were launched by Eclipse. Use it to pause program execution, view tracebacks, and locate the cause of deadlocks (more on this shortly). Table 12 shows the commands on the Debug view's toolbar.

Table 12. Debug view toolbar

Icon	Description
▣▶	Continue running a program or thread that was previously paused.
▢▢	Pause the current program or thread.
▣	Terminate the current program.
ᴺ͵	Disconnect from a remote debugger.
✖	Remove all record of previously terminated programs.
ᴿ͵	Single step into method calls.
◌	Single step over method calls.
ᵿ	Continue execution until the current method returns.
▤	Rewind execution to the beginning of the selected stack frame (requires VM support).
ᴾ͵	Enable/disable step filters (toggle).

Step filters prevent you from having to stop in classes, packages, initializers, or constructors that you don't find interesting. The list of filters is configured in Window → Preferences → Java → Debug → Step Filtering.

One option in the Debug view menu deserves a special mention: Show Monitors. *Monitors* are Java thread synchronization points. *Deadlocks* occur when one thread is waiting on a monitor that will never be released. When you turn on the Show Monitors option, the Debug view will display a list of monitors owned or waited on by each thread. Any deadlocks will be highlighted.

Declaration View

The Declaration view (in the Java perspective) shows the Java source code that defined the current selection. Use this view to see the declaration of types and members as you move around your code, without having to switch editors. The toolbar for the Declaration view contains the single icon shown in Table 13.

Table 13. Declaration view toolbar

Icon	Description
⬚	Open an editor on the input source code.

TIP

The declaration can also be seen by holding down the Ctrl key and hovering the mouse pointer over the type or member in the Java editor.

Display View

The Display view (in the Debug perspective) shows expression results in an unstructured format. Use it as a temporary work area in which to place expressions and calculate their values. Table 14 shows the commands on the Display view's toolbar.

Table 14. Display view toolbar

Icon	Description
🔍	Inspect the selected expression.
🗊	Display the selected expression.
⚙	Evaluate the selected expression.
🗎	Erase everything in the Display view.

There are four different ways to evaluate expressions in the Eclipse debugger:

*Inspect (*Ctrl+Shift+I *or* Run → Inspect*)*
> Show the value of an expression in an expandable tree format. Optionally, copy it into the Expressions view. The value is never recalculated.

*Display (*Ctrl+Shift+D *or* Run → Display*)*
> Show the value of an expression in a simple string format. Optionally, copy it into the Display view. The value is never recalculated.

*Execute (*Ctrl+U *or* Run → Execute*)*
> Evaluate the expression but don't show its value.

*Watch (*Run → Watch*)*
> Copy an expression into the Expressions view. Its value is recalculated every time you do a Step or Resume command.

For example, in the Java editor, you could highlight an expression such as array[i-1] and press Ctrl+Shift+D. A pop-up window appears, showing the current value of that array element. Press Ctrl+Shift+D again and the expression is copied to the Display view.

If this view looks familiar to you, that's because it's essentially an unnamed scrapbook page.

TIP

See the "Scrapbook Pages" section in Part V for more information on scrapbook pages.

Error Log View

The Error Log view is not included by default in any perspective, but you can open it with Window → Show View → Error Log. Use it to view internal Eclipse errors and stack dumps when reporting problems to the developers. It can also display warnings and informational messages logged by Eclipse plug-ins. Table 15 shows the commands on the Error Log view's toolbar.

Table 15. Error Log view toolbar

Icon	Description
	Export the error log to another file.
	Import the error log from another file.
	Clear the view without modifying the logfile.
	Clear the view and erase the logfile.
	Open the logfile in an external text editor.
	Reload the view with the contents of the logfile.

TIP

See "Reporting Bugs" in Part IX for instructions on how to report problems in Eclipse.

Expressions View

The Expressions view (in the Debug perspective) shows a list of expressions and their values in the debugger. Use it to examine program states persistently as you step through your code, and to set breakpoints when fields are accessed or modified. This view is similar to the Variables view (described later in Part VII) except that the Expressions view shows only expressions that you have explicitly added. Table 16 describes the Expressions view's toolbar.

Table 16. Expressions view toolbar

Icon	Description
	Show full type names (toggle).
	Show logical structure (toggle).

Table 16. Expressions view toolbar (continued)

Icon	Description
⊟	Collapse all the expanded trees in the view.
✖	Remove the current expression from the view.
✖	Remove all expressions in the view.

There are three ways of looking at any expression in the Eclipse IDE; this is true for both the Expressions view and the Variables view:

Literal mode
  The fields, and nothing but the fields

Logical mode
  The way you normally think about the object

Details pane
  The string representation (as returned by the toString( ) method)

Consider a java.lang.LinkedList object. If you look at it literally (as in Figure 26), you'll see it contains some internal data structures, such as the number of items and a reference to the first item. But if you look at it logically (Figure 27), it simply contains a list of objects.

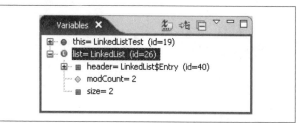

Figure 26. Literal mode shows an object's internal data structures.

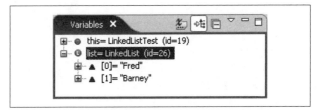

Figure 27. Logical mode shows what the object really means.

Additionally, the Expressions and Variables views support an optional text area called the Details pane. This pane shows the string representation of the selected item (see Figure 28). Use the view menu to arrange the panes horizontally or vertically, or to disable the Details pane altogether.

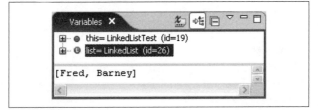

Figure 28. The Details pane shows an object's string representation.

TIP

You can create your own ways of looking at expressions by defining new Logical Structures and Detail Formatters in the debugger preferences (Window → Preferences → Java → Debug).

Hierarchy View

The Hierarchy view (in the Java perspective) shows the supertypes and subtypes for the selected Java object. Use it to explore the type hierarchy, fields, and methods for a class or interface by selecting the type in the Java editor or Package Explorer view and pressing F4 (Navigate → Open Type Hierarchy).

The Hierarchy view has two panes, each with its own toolbar. The top pane is the Type Hierarchy tree (see Table 17), which lists the object's supertypes and subtypes. The optional bottom pane is the Member list (Table 18). It shows fields and methods. Double-click on any type or member to edit its source code.

Table 17. Type Hierarchy toolbar

Icon	Description
	Show the type hierarchy from object down.
	Show the supertype hierarchy from the current type up.
	Show the subtype hierarchy from the current type down.
	View a previous type in the history.

Table 18. Member list toolbar

Icon	Description
	Lock the member list and show inherited members in the Type Hierarchy pane (toggle).
	Show all inherited members (toggle).
	Sort members by defining type (toggle).
	Show/hide fields (toggle).
	Show/hide statics (toggle).
	Show/hide nonpublic members (toggle).

TIP

Press Ctrl+T in the Java editor to show the type hierarchy in a searchable pop-up window.

Javadoc View

The Javadoc view (in the Java perspective) shows Java documentation from comments at the definition of the current selection. Use it if you need a larger, permanent version of the pop-up window you get when you hover the mouse pointer over a type or member in the Java editor. The toolbar for the Javadoc view contains the single icon shown in Table 19.

Table 19. Javadoc view toolbar

Icon	Description
	Open the input source code.

Like Hover Help, the Javadoc view requires access to the source code.

TIP

See "Hover Help" in Part VI for more information.

JUnit View

The JUnit view (in the Java perspective) shows the progress and results of JUnit tests. Use it to see what tests failed and why (see Part V for instructions on how to run unit tests).

The JUnit view has two panes, each with its own toolbar. The JUnit tests pane (see Table 20 for toolbar commands) lists the tests that failed (or a hierarchy of all tests). When you select a failed test in this pane, the Failure trace pane (see Table 21 for toolbar commands) shows a traceback pinpointing where the failure occurred. Double-click on any test name, class name, or traceback line to edit the source code at that point.

Table 20. JUnit tests toolbar

Icon	Description
⬇	Go to the next failed test.
⬆	Go to the previous failed test.
■	Stop the current test run.
🔍	Rerun all tests.
🔍	Rerun just the tests that failed.
🔒	Keep the test list from scrolling.

Table 21. Failure trace toolbar

Icon	Description
⇥	Filter unwanted stack frames from failure tracebacks.
⬜	Compare the expected and actual values on a JUnit assertion (string values only).

Use the JUnit preference page (Window → Preferences → Java → JUnit) to configure the list of stack frames to filter out.

Navigator View

The Navigator view (in the Resource perspective) shows all projects in the workspace as they exist on disk. Use it to see the literal directories and files. Contrast this with the Package Explorer view, which shows a Java-centric representation. Table 22 describes the Navigator view's toolbar.

Table 22. Navigator view toolbar

Icon	Description
⇦	Go back in the navigator history.
⇨	Go forward in the navigator history.
⬆	Go up to the parent directory.
▤	Collapse all the expanded trees in this view.
⬆	Link selections with the editor.

Right-click on a directory and select Go Into to focus on that directory. Then you can use the Back, Forward, and Up toolbar buttons to move around in the tree.

Outline View

The Outline view (in the Java and Debug perspectives) shows a tree representation of the resource being edited. Use it to quickly find the major elements of your class and study the overall API you have designed. In order for the outline to appear, the current editor must support it. Table 23 describes the Outline view's toolbar.

Table 23. Outline toolbar

Icon	Description
↓^a_z	Sort members alphabetically (toggle).
🔖	Show/hide fields (toggle).
⚑^{s}	Show/hide statics (toggle).
●	Show/hide nonpublic members (toggle).
⚑^{t}	Show/hide local types (toggle).

TIP

Press Ctrl+O in the Java editor to show the outline in a searchable pop-up window.

Package Explorer View

The Package Explorer view (in the Java perspective) shows all projects in the workspace using logical Java groupings. Use it as your primary window into the world of your Java source code. Table 24 shows the Package Explorer view's toolbar.

Table 24. Package Explorer toolbar

Icon	Description
⇦	Go back in the Package Explorer history.
⇨	Go forward in the Package Explorer history.
⬆	Go up to the parent directory.
⊟	Collapse all the expanded trees in this view.
⮎	Link selections with the editor.

The Package Explorer view is a much more powerful version of the Navigator view, custom tailored for Java development. The main difference is that the Package Explorer understands Java source directories and packages. For example, suppose your project has a package named a.b.c. You will see the package a.b.c in the Package Explorer view, while in the Navigator view, you will see the directory tree (a containing b containing c).

Views such as the Package Explorer support thousands of icon variations made from combining *base icons* (for simple objects like packages and files) with *decorator icons*, also known as *decorations* (for errors, warnings, accessibility, etc.). Tables 25 and 26 show a few of the common icons you should become familiar with.

Table 25. Common base icons

Icon	Description
📁	Project
▦	Source folder
📂	Plain folder
📚	Java library
⊞	Java package
🄹	Java file
🄹	Scrapbook page
📦	Class file

Table 25. Common base icons (continued)

Icon	Description
	JAR file
	Plain file
	Java class
	Java interface
	Public method
	Private method
	Protected method
	Public field
	Private field
	Protected field

Table 26. Common decorations

Icon	Description
	Error
	Warning
	Version controlled
	Inherited
/	Deprecated
A	Abstract
C	Constructor
F	Final
J	Java related
S	Static

Problems View

The Problems view (in the Java perspective) shows all the errors and warnings in the workspace. Double-click on a line in this view to jump directly to the offending source line. Table 27 describes the Problems view toolbar.

Table 27. Problems view toolbar

Icon	Description
✖	Delete the selected problem(s).
⇶	Filter out some problems.

TIP

You'll often want to use a filter to see just the problems for the current project or perhaps just the currently selected resource.

Right-click on a problem to see a context menu. One of the options there is Quick Fix (Ctrl+1). Use this to quickly repair common errors.

TIP

See "Quick Fixes" in Part VI for more information.

Search View

The Search view (in the Java perspective) shows the results of any search operation. Use it to filter and select just the matches you're interested in. Table 28 describes the Search view toolbar.

Table 28. Search view toolbar

Icon	Description
⬇	Go to next match.
⬆	Go to previous match.
✖	Remove selected match(es) from the view.
✖	Remove all matches from the view.
⊞	Expand the search tree.
⊟	Collapse the search tree.

Table 28. Search view toolbar (continued)

Icon	Description
■	Stop a running search.
🔄	Go back to a previous search in the history.
📁	Group by project.
🗂	Group by package.
📄	Group by file.
👥	Group by type.

The Search view can show its results in either *flat mode* (a plain listing) or *hierarchical mode* (an expandable tree). The grouping actions in the toolbar are only available in hierarchical mode. Use the View menu to change modes.

Tasks View

The Tasks view (in the Java perspective) lists all the markers placed in your source code. *Markers* are reminders that you or Eclipse add to the code to indicate something that needs your attention later. They can be added manually (Edit → Add Bookmark... or Edit → Add Task...), but more commonly the compiler adds them when it encounters a special comment in your code like this:

```
// TODO: Revisit this later
```

The comment strings TODO, FIXME, and XXX are recognized by default. Add any others that you commonly use in your code to Window → Preferences → Java → Compiler → Task Tags.

Table 29 describes the Tasks view toolbar.

Table 29. Tasks view toolbar

Icon	Description
◁▤	Create a new task.
✖	Delete the selected task(s).
⇉▷	Filter out some tasks.

Variables View

The Variables view (in the Debug perspective) shows all the parameters and local variables in scope during a debugging session. Use this view to keep an eye on your program's state as you step through it. The Variables view toolbar is described in Table 30.

Table 30. Variables view toolbar

Icon	Description
🐛	Show full type names (toggle).
⇌≣	Show logical structure (toggle).
▤	Collapse all the expanded trees in the view.

TIP

If you're currently stopped in a nonstatic method, the first item in the Variables view will be this. Expand it to see your instance variables.

PART VIII

Short Takes

This pocket guide wouldn't fit in your pocket if it described every nuance of Eclipse in detail. However, I want to briefly mention a few more of Eclipse's notable features in this part of the book. Some of these are built into the Eclipse SDK; some are plug-ins that you need to download and install yourself.

TIP

The packaging of Eclipse is constantly evolving, so by the time you read this, you may be able to find downloads that combine parts of the Eclipse SDK with plug-ins for a specific task—for example, web development.

In addition, you can find hundreds of plug-ins that extend Eclipse by searching the community web sites listed in Part IX.

To find out more about any of these features, see the online help topic or web sites listed in the following sections. Note that when you install a plug-in, it will often add a new section to the Help Contents that explains how to use it.

CVS

CVS is a popular source management system for projects and teams of any size. You use a *CVS repository* to hold the evolving versions of your code, tools, scripts, documentation, and so forth. The Eclipse IDE comes with excellent CVS integration—which makes sense, as CVS is currently used in the development of all Eclipse projects.

Use the CVS Repository Exploring perspective to see the contents of a CVS repository. There you can define the server location, and view or *check out* (make a local copy of) the code. Eclipse provides a variety of options to keep your local copy up to date with repository changes, including additional views in the Team Synchronizing perspective. A terrific compare and merge utility (one of my favorite features in Eclipse) makes handling conflicts easy.

A history of all changes for a specific file (resource) can be seen in the CVS Resource History view. Double-click on a line in this view to open an editor on that revision, or select two revisions, right-click, and select the Compare command to see their differences. Another useful CVS command is Show Annotation. This lets you scroll through a particular file and see who touched each line, when, and why.

Online help
> Help → Help Contents → Workbench User Guide → Concepts → Team programming with CVS

Web sites
> *http://www.cvshome.org*
> *http://dev.eclipse.org*

Ant

Ant is the Java-based successor to the venerable *make* tool. You can use Ant for automating almost any development task, from compiling to testing to packaging and deployment. Eclipse can import and export Ant-based projects, edit Ant files, and run Ant tasks manually or as part of a build process. Next to the Java editor, the Ant editor is one of the most advanced editors available in the IDE, with support for code assist, outlining, and formatting.

Online help
> Help → Help Contents → Workbench User Guide →
> Concepts → External tools → Ant support

Web sites
> http://ant.apache.org
>
> http://cruisecontrol.sourceforge.net

Web Tools Platform

Do you write web pages, edit XML, develop Java servlets, or dream about EJB? Then the Web Tools Platform (WTP) project is for you. This is a separate download that—when installed—integrates into your Eclipse SDK installation.

There are two parts to the WTP: web standard tools (covering HTML, XML, XSD, etc.) and Java standard tools (for JSPs, EJBs, and so forth). This project supports web service development, server management, debugging code on the server, and more.

Web site
> http://www.eclipse.org/webtools

Testing and Performance

The Test and Performance Tools Platform (TPTP—who makes up these acronyms?) provides tools and technologies that bring together traditional profiling, monitoring, tracing, and testing. For example, you can use it to correlate CPU usage on one machine with events logged by another.

Web site
> http://www.eclipse.org/tptp

Visual Editor

The Visual Editor project lets you create graphical user interfaces for your programs. It supports *round-tripping*, which means you can edit your interface in visual mode (using drag-and-drop), switch to source mode to make a few changes, switch back, and continue seamlessly.

Web site
  http://www.eclipse.org/ve

C/C++ Development

Java isn't the only language that the Eclipse IDE supports. The C/C++ Development Toolkit (CDT) comes with everything you need for C/C++ development except the tool chain itself (i.e., the compiler, linker, and debugger). CDT works with a variety of tools from various embedded systems vendors; for ordinary desktop applications, you can download and use the free *gcc* compiler and *gdb* debugger from the GNU project.

Web sites
  http://www.eclipse.org/cdt
  http://www.gnu.org

AspectJ

The Eclipse project is the home of AspectJ, an aspect-oriented extension to the Java language, along with the AspectJ Development Toolkit (AJDT), which integrates the language into the Eclipse IDE. AspectJ provides clean modularization of crosscutting concerns such as error checking, monitoring, and logging. A related project, the Concern Manipulation Environment (CME), aims to bring some elements of aspect programming to pure Java.

Web sites
   http://www.eclipse.org/aspectj
   http://www.eclipse.org/cme

Plug-in Development

Under the covers, Eclipse is a completely modular system
with dozens—if not hundreds—of plug-ins working together
on top of a small dynamic runtime. Each plug-in defines
public extension points, which are like the sockets on a
power strip. Other plug-ins contribute extensions that, well,
plug into those sockets. Thus the system organically grows
functionality as more plug-ins are added. At the same time,
the runtime is scalable, so you never have to worry about
blowing a fuse.

The Plug-in Development Environment (PDE) bundled with
the Eclipse SDK lets you define your own plug-ins in order to
extend Eclipse. PDE supports defining and using extension
points, debugging your plug-ins, packaging, and more.

TIP

The source code for Eclipse is freely available; in fact, it's
bundled with the SDK package you installed. This is a
great resource for learning plug-in programming. File →
Import → External Plug-ins and Fragments brings parts of
the code into your workspace.

Online help
   Help → Help Contents → Platform Plug-in Developer
   Guide

Web sites
   http://www.eclipse.org/articles
   http://www.ibm.com/developerworks

Rich Client Platform

Because of the flexible open source license under which Eclipse is released, you can use Eclipse code and technologies in your own programs, even if they are not open source. A subset of the Eclipse SDK called the Rich Client Platform (RCP) provides basic functionality common to most desktop applications, such as windowing and menu support, online help, user preferences, and more. By building your own custom application on top of this framework, you can cut the development time of your projects significantly.

Since Eclipse technology is all based on plug-ins, the PDE is used to write RCP programs. You can brand your applications with custom icons, window titles, and a splash screen, and you can deploy them via traditional zip files, professional installers, or even JNLP. A number of templates and tutorials are available.

Online help
> Help → Help Contents → Platform Plug-in Developer Guide → Building a Rich Client Platform application

Web sites
> *http://www.eclipse.org/rcp*
>
> *http://www.eclipse.org/legal*
>
> *http://www.eclipsepowered.org*

Standard Widget Toolkit

The Eclipse user interface is written in Java using the Standard Widget Toolkit (SWT). SWT uses the native facilities of your operating system to achieve high performance and fidelity indistinguishable from that of C-based applications. You can use the same toolkit for your own applications.

SWT is one of the three main GUI toolkits supported by Java. The other two are AWT and Swing. SWT provides limited interoperability with these, allowing you to host AWT and Swing controls inside a SWT application. On Windows, SWT can even host ActiveX and .NET controls. SWT is unique in its ability to bring these worlds together.

A framework called JFace is often used with SWT to provide higher-level concepts, such as viewers, actions, and wizards. Both SWT and JFace are included with the Eclipse SDK and RCP packages.

Online help
> Help → Help Contents → Platform Plug-in Developer Guide → Standard Widget Toolkit

Web site
> http://www.eclipse.org/swt

PART IX

Help and Community

Welcome to the Eclipse community. Membership is free, and you've already taken the first steps by installing the software and reading this guide. To help you go further, online help, web sites, articles, and other resources are available to assist you, as are thousands of Eclipse enthusiasts from around the world.

Online Help

Eclipse provides an extensible *online help* system with details about the version of Eclipse you're using and any plug-ins you have installed. It can be searched and viewed in several different ways.

Getting Help

The most common way to view online help is to select Help → Help Contents. A separate Help window will open, showing several help topics. Expand the topics to hone in on the information you need, or enter a keyword in the Search field at the top of the window.

Another way to get help is with *dynamic help*. To use dynamic help, simply press F1 (or select Help → Dynamic Help) and an embedded Help view will appear. As your focus changes to different views and editors, the Help content is updated to show help for what you are doing at the moment. Select Help → Search Help… to find help topics relevant to the view you're currently in.

Help Topics

If you install the Eclipse SDK as detailed in Part I, you will find the following topics listed in the Help contents:

Workbench User Guide
> Contains information on how to use the IDE in general, independent of your programming language.

Java Development User Guide
> Discusses how to use the Java language support (editors, views, etc.) provided by Eclipse.

Platform Plug-in Developer Guide
> Covers the concepts and programming interfaces used to write Eclipse plug-ins.

JDT Plug-in Developer Guide
> Covers writing plug-ins specifically for the Java Development Tools.

PDE Guide
> Describes how to use the plug-in development environment included in the Eclipse SDK.

TIP

Depending on your options, some of these topics may be hidden. Click the Show All Topics button to see them all.

Eclipse Web Site

The official Eclipse web site, *http://www.eclipse.org*, is your best source of information on Eclipse: the platform, the IDE, and the community. The design of this site may change over time, but as of this writing, the major sections are:

About us

Learn about the Eclipse project, how it got started, who is involved in it, how the governance works, legal questions, logo programs, and so forth.

Projects

Eclipse development is split into top-level projects, subprojects, and components. On the Projects page, you can see how all this is organized. Drill down to get to FAQs, documentation, source code, etc.

Download

This area should be familiar from Part I. It's where you'll find the latest prebuilt versions of Eclipse.

Articles

The articles section is full of technical information for developers using or extending Eclipse. Consider writing an article yourself to add to the community knowledge base.

Newsgroups

The main user forums are found here (see the "Newsgroups" section, later in this chapter).

Community

This is where you'll find out about conferences, user groups, web sites, books, courses, free and commercial plug-ins, awards, and much more.

Search

Locate any page at *eclipse.org*, including newsgroup and mailing list archives.

Bugs

Find or report bugs and enhancement requests.

Community Web Sites

Many individuals and companies have created web sites to address particular needs of the community. Here are a few of the most popular ones. More can be found in the Community Resources area of the *eclipse.org* web site.

EclipseZone (http://www.eclipsezone.com)
> An online community by and for Eclipse users everywhere.

Planet Eclipse (http://planeteclipse.org)
> Planet Eclipse is a window into the world, work, and lives of Eclipse users and contributors.

Plug-ins Registry (http://eclipse-plugins.info)
> This is a nonprofit registry of Eclipse plug-ins, created and maintained by Eclipse users.

Eclipse Plugin Central (http://eclipseplugincentral.com)
> This site offers a plug-in directory, reviews, ratings, news, forums, and listings for products and services.

Eclipse Wiki (http://eclipse-wiki.info)
> This user-editable web site has FAQs, tips, tricks, and other useful information.

IBM AlphaWorks (http://alphaworks.ibm.com/eclipse)
> Part of IBM's emerging technologies web site, this is dedicated to Eclipse and WebSphere-related projects and plug-ins.

IBM developerWorks (http://ibm.com/developerworks/opensource)
> developerWorks hosts a variety of tutorials, articles, and related information on Eclipse and other open source projects.

Apache (http://www.apache.org)
> Apache software is used throughout Eclipse, and the two projects collaborate in many areas.

Source Forge (http://sf.net)
   A large and growing number of Eclipse plug-ins are being developed in this open source nexus.

O'Reilly Open Source (http://opensource.oreilly.com)
   This O'Reilly Resource Center provides a broad range of references and links to publications about open source.

Reporting Bugs

The single most important way you can contribute to the Eclipse community is to report every bug you find, so they can be fixed. All software has bugs, but too often users do not take the time to report them. Your ideas for enhancements are also valuable.

Bug reports and enhancement requests are both stored at *eclipse.org* in an open source tracking system called Bugzilla. The only difference between the entries for the two is that all enhancement requests are marked with a severity of "enhancement" (in Bugzilla, "bug report" refers to both types of entries).

TIP

Remember to always use the most recent milestone or stable version of Eclipse you can find. Why? With a current release, you shorten the time between when a bug slips in and when you report that bug, making it much easier to diagnose and fix the problem.

To report a bug or request an enhancement, first go to the Eclipse home page (*http://www.eclipse.org*) and select the "bugs" link. The first time you use Bugzilla, you'll need to create an account.

New Account

Although you can search the database without a Bugzilla account, you'll need one to add or modify any entries. Click the "Create a Bugzilla account" link, enter your email address and name, and click the "submit" button. The system will create the account and send a confirmation by email.

Searching

Before creating a new Bugzilla entry, take a moment to search the database to see if someone else has beaten you to it. From the main Bugs page, select the "Find a bug report" link, then enter one or more words in either the Summary field or the Comment field, and click Search.

If you find an entry that matches your problem or request, add yourself to the cc list—a list of email addresses that get copied on any modification to the entry. You may also wish to vote for the issue in order to indicate your interest. Votes don't determine priority by themselves, but they sometimes do factor in.

Adding an Entry

If you can't find an existing Bugzilla entry, you'll need to create a new one. From the main Bugs page, select "Report a new bug" or "Enter an enhancement/feature request."

Next, you'll be prompted for the project. If you're using the Eclipse SDK, the choice is simple: for anything relating specifically to Java development, pick JDT; otherwise, pick Platform.

On the next page, select a component. If you're not sure, click on the "help" link or just take a guess. Enter a one-line description of the issue in the Summary field and a more detailed description in the Description field. When reporting a bug, supply the steps that someone else will need to follow to reproduce the problem.

Often when there's a bug in Eclipse, the system will record an event in the Eclipse error log. This record contains important information that can help the developers diagnose the problem. Locate the event in the Error Log view (discussed in Part VII) and paste it at the end of the Description field. Click the Commit button to complete the report.

At the time of this writing, I've personally entered 367 bug reports, including 106 enhancement requests; 268 of these entries have been resolved. In addition, I'm cc'd on 437 bugs and have commented on 659. While you might not become that involved, I challenge you to play your part in improving Eclipse.

Newsgroups

Eclipse user forums are hosted on *eclipse.org* using ordinary newsgroups. All newsgroup content is protected by a password in order to control spam. To get the password, go to the Eclipse home page and select the "newsgroups/user forum" link; you should see a link to request a password. Submit your information and the password will be mailed to you.

Although there is a web-based interface for the forums, the best way to participate is to use a rich client news reader, such as Thunderbird (*http://www.mozilla.org/products/thunderbird*). Enter the news server name (*news.eclipse.org*), the userid, and the password in the appropriate place for your reader.

Here are a few newsgroups that I recommend you start with:

eclipse.newcomer
Ask questions about downloading, installing, and getting started with Eclipse in this newsgroup.

eclipse.platform
Come here to participate in technical discussions about how to use or extend Eclipse.

eclipse.platform.jdt
> This group is for technical discussions about how to use the Java Development Tools.

eclipse.foundation
> This forum is for general discussions pertaining to the Eclipse Foundation and its communities and governance.

eclipse.commercial
> This group is intended to allow commercial vendors to post product releases and information about commercial products based on Eclipse.

Mailing Lists

For the most part, mailing lists at *eclipse.org* are intended for use by developers working on day-to-day development of Eclipse itself. The development mailing lists are the way design and implementation issues are discussed and decisions voted on by the committers (developers who've earned write access to the source repository).

Anyone can listen in, but questions and discussions about using Eclipse and Eclipse-based tools or developing plug-ins should be posted to one of the newsgroups listed previously.

Conclusion

Eclipse is not just an IDE for Java developers, though that's how most people are introduced to it. Eclipse technology is used by everyone from office secretaries running custom RCP applications to NASA scientists planning Mars Rover missions (seriously!). From the hobbyist to the professional, from casual users to committers, Eclipse appeals to all of us for different reasons, but we're all part of the community, and we all have something important to contribute. See you online.

Commands

Eclipse supports over 350 commands for all aspects of editing, running, and debugging programs. Most of these can be found on a menu—or submenu—inside Eclipse, while some are bound to keystrokes. Then there are the ones that are not normally accessible at all. In order to run those, you must first bind them to a key (Window → Preferences → General → Keys).

TIP

Press Ctrl+Shift+L (Help → Key Assist…) to see a quick list of the currently defined keys.

This appendix lists most of the commands available in Eclipse along with their key bindings and menu paths (if any). Commands are organized into categories such as Edit and File, just as you would see them listed in the Keys Preferences. Within each category, the commands are listed in alphabetical order. The format used is:

Command [Default key bindings]

Main menu path

Some commands can be accessed by two or more equivalent key sequences. For example, the Copy command's key bindings are listed as "Ctrl+C | Ctrl+Insert." The vertical bar indicates that either Ctrl+C or Ctrl+Insert will work.

Other bindings are actually composed of two keys pressed in sequence. For example, the key binding for "Quick Assist - Rename in file" is shown as "Ctrl+2, R." The comma indicates you should press Ctrl+2, release, and then press the R key.

TIP

It sounds more complicated than it really is. If you press the first key of a multikey sequence and pause, a window will appear to remind you what to press next.

In the interest of space, only key bindings for the default configuration on Windows are listed. Keys for other platforms are similar, and you should be able to infer these for yourself. An Emacs-like configuration is also selectable from the Keys Preferences. Someone has even written a plug-in that supports *vi*-style keystrokes (search for it on the plug-in sites listed in the "Community Web Sites" section in Part IX).

Edit Commands

Add Bookmark [No key binding]
Edit → Add Bookmark...

Add Task [No key binding]
Edit → Add Task...

Content Assist [Ctrl+Space]
Edit → Content Assist

Context Information [Ctrl+Shift+Space]
Edit → Parameter Hints

Copy [Ctrl+C | Ctrl+Insert]
Edit → Copy

Cut [Ctrl+X | Shift+Delete]

Edit → Cut

Delete [Delete]

Edit → Delete

Find and Replace [Ctrl+F]

Edit → Find/Replace…

Find Next [Ctrl+K]

Edit → Find Next

Find Previous [Ctrl+Shift+K]

Edit → Find Previous

Incremental Find [Ctrl+J]

Edit → Incremental Find Next

Incremental Find Reverse [Ctrl+Shift+J]

Edit → Incremental Find Previous

Paste [Ctrl+V | Shift+Insert]

Edit → Paste

Quick Diff Toggle [Ctrl+Shift+Q]

(No menu)

Quick Fix [Ctrl+1]

Edit → Quick Fix

Redo [Ctrl+Y]

Edit → Redo

Restore Last Selection [Alt+Shift+Down]

Edit → Expand Selection To → Restore Last Selection

Revert Line [No key binding]

(No menu)

Revert Lines [No key binding]

(No menu)

Revert to Saved [No key binding]

File → Revert

Select All [Ctrl+A]

Edit → Select All

Select Enclosing Element [Alt+Shift+Up]

Edit → Expand Selection To → Enclosing Element

Select Next Element [Alt+Shift+Right]

Edit → Expand Selection To → Next Element

Select Previous Element [Alt+Shift+Left]

Edit → Expand Selection To → Previous Element

Shift Left [No key binding]

Source → Shift Left

Shift Right [No key binding]

Source → Shift Right

Show Line Numbers [No key binding]

(No menu)

Show Tooltip Description [F2]

Edit → Show Tooltip Description

Toggle Insert Mode [Ctrl+Shift+Insert]

Edit → Smart Insert Mode

Undo [Ctrl+Z]

Edit → Undo

Word Completion [Alt+/]

Edit → Word Completion

File Commands

Close [Ctrl+F4 | Ctrl+W]

> File → Close

Close All [Ctrl+Shift+F4 | Ctrl+Shift+W]

> File → Close All

Convert Line Delimiters to Mac OS 9 [No key binding]

> File → Convert Line Delimiters To → Mac OS 9

Convert Line Delimiters to Unix [No key binding]

> File → Convert Line Delimiters To → Unix

Convert Line Delimiters to Windows [No key binding]

> File → Convert Line Delimiters To → Windows

Exit [No key binding]

> File → Exit

Export [No key binding]

> File → Export…

Import [No key binding]

> File → Import…

Move [No key binding]

> File → Move…

New [Ctrl+N]

> File → New → Other…

New menu [Alt+Shift+N]

> File → New

Open File… [No key binding]

> File → Open File…

Open Workspace [No key binding]

> File → Switch Workspace…

Print [Ctrl+P]

> File → Print…

Properties [Alt+Enter]

> File → Properties

Refresh [F5]

> File → Refresh

Remove Trailing Whitespace [No key binding]

> (No menu)

Rename [F2]

> File → Rename…

Revert [No key binding]

> File → Revert

Save [Ctrl+S]

> File → Save

Save All [Ctrl+Shift+S]

> File → Save All

Save As [No key binding]

> File → Save As…

Help Commands

About [No key binding]

> Help → About

Dynamic Help [F1]

> Help → Dynamic Help

Help Contents [No key binding]

   Help → Help Contents

Help Search [No key binding]

   Help → Search Help…

Tips and Tricks [No key binding]

   Help → Tips and Tricks…

Welcome [No key binding]

   Help → Welcome…

Navigate Commands

Back [No key binding]

   Navigate → Go To → Back

Backward History [Alt+Left]

   Navigate → Back

Forward [No key binding]

   Navigate → Go To → Forward

Forward History [Alt+Right]

   Navigate → Forward

Go Into [No key binding]

   Navigate → Go Into

Go to Line [Ctrl+L]

   Navigate → Go to Line…

Go to Matching Bracket [Ctrl+Shift+P]

   Navigate → Go To → Matching Bracket

Go to Next Member [Ctrl+Shift+Down]

   Navigate → Go To → Next Member

Go to Package [No key binding]

Navigate → Go To → Package...

Go to Previous Member [Ctrl+Shift+Up]

Navigate → Go To → Previous Member

Go to Resource [No key binding]

Navigate → Go To → Resource...

Go to Type [No key binding]

Navigate → Go To → Type...

Last Edit Location [Ctrl+Q]

Navigate → Last Edit Location

Next [Ctrl+.]

Navigate → Next

Open Call Hierarchy [Ctrl+Alt+H]

Navigate → Open Call Hierarchy

Open Declaration [F3]

Navigate → Open Declaration

Open External Javadoc [Shift+F2]

Navigate → Open External Javadoc

Open Resource [Ctrl+Shift+R]

Navigate → Open Resource...

Open Structure [Ctrl+F3]

(No menu)

Open Super Implementation [No key binding]

Navigate → Open Super Implementation

Open Type [Ctrl+Shift+T]

Navigate → Open Type...

Open Type Hierarchy [F4]

Navigate → Open Type Hierarchy

Open Type in Hierarchy [Ctrl+Shift+H]

Navigate → Open Type in Hierarchy…

Previous [Ctrl+,]

Navigate → Previous

Quick Hierarchy [Ctrl+T]

Navigate → Quick Type Hierarchy

Quick Outline [Ctrl+O]

Navigate → Quick Outline

Show in Menu [Alt+Shift+W]

Navigate → Show In

Show in Package Explorer [No key binding]

Navigate → Show In → Package Explorer

Up [No key binding]

Navigate → Go To → Up One [Level

Perspective Commands

CVS Repository Exploring [No key binding]

Window → Open Perspective → Other… → CVS Repository Exploring

Debug [No key binding]

Window → Open Perspective → Debug

Java [No key binding]

Window → Open Perspective → Java

Java Browsing [No key binding]

Window → Open Perspective → Java Browsing

Java Type Hierarchy [No key binding]

Window → Open Perspective → Other… → Java Type Hierarchy

Team Synchronizing [No key binding]

Window → Open Perspective → Other… → Team Synchronizing

Project Commands

Build All [Ctrl+B]

Project → Build All

Build Clean [No key binding]

Project → Clean…

Build Project [No key binding]

Project → Build Project

Close Project [No key binding]

Project → Close Project

Generate Javadoc [No key binding]

Project → Generate Javadoc…

Open Project [No key binding]

Project → Open Project

Properties [No key binding]

Project → Properties

Rebuild All [No key binding]

(No menu)

Rebuild Project [No key binding]

(No menu)

Repeat Working Set Build [No key binding]

(No menu)

Refactor Commands

Change Method Signature [Alt+Shift+C]

Refactor → Change Method Signature…

Convert Anonymous Class to Nested [No key binding]

Refactor → Convert Anonymous Class to Nested…

Convert Local Variable to Field [Alt+Shift+F]

Refactor → Convert Local Variable to Field…

Encapsulate Field [No key binding]

Refactor → Encapsulate Field…

Extract Constant [No key binding]

Refactor → Extract Constant…

Extract Interface [No key binding]

Refactor → Extract Interface…

Extract Local Variable [Alt+Shift+L]

Refactor → Extract Local Variable…

Extract Method [Alt+Shift+M]

Refactor → Extract Method…

Generalize Type [No key binding]

Refactor → Generalize Type…

Infer Generic Type Arguments [No key binding]

Refactor → Infer Generic Type Arguments…

Inline [Alt+Shift+I]

Refactor → Inline…

Introduce Factory [No key binding]

Refactor → Introduce Factory…

Introduce Parameter [No key binding]

Refactor → Introduce Parameter…

Move - Refactoring [Alt+Shift+V]

Refactor → Move…

Move Member Type to New File [No key binding]

Refactor → Move Member Type to New File…

Pull Up [No key binding]

Refactor → Pull Up…

Push Down [No key binding]

Refactor → Push Down…

Rename - Refactoring [Alt+Shift+R]

Refactor → Rename…

Show Refactor Quick Menu [Alt+Shift+T]

(No menu)

Use Supertype Where Possible [No key binding]

Refactor → Use Supertype Where Possible

Run/Debug Commands

Add Class Load Breakpoint [No key binding]

Run → Add Class Load Breakpoint…

Add Java Exception Breakpoint [No key binding]

Run → Add Java Exception Breakpoint…

Debug Ant Build [Alt+Shift+D, Q]

Run → Debug…

Debug Eclipse Application [Alt+Shift+D, E]

Run → Debug…

Debug Java Applet [Alt+Shift+D, A]

Run → Debug…

Debug Java Application [Alt+Shift+D, J]

Run → Debug…

Debug JUnit Plug-in Test [Alt+Shift+D, P]

Run → Debug…

Debug JUnit Test [Alt+Shift+D, T]

Run → Debug…

Debug Last Launched [F11]

Run → Debug Last Launched

Debug SWT Application [Alt+Shift+D, S]

Run → Debug…

Debug … [No key binding]

Run → Debug…

Display [Ctrl+Shift+D]

Run → Display

EOF [Ctrl+Z]

(No menu)
(Console view only)

Execute [Ctrl+U]

Run → Execute

External Tools... [No key binding]

> Run → External Tools → External Tools...

Inspect [Ctrl+Shift+I]

> Run → Inspect

Profile Last Launched [No key binding]

> Run → Profile Last Launched

Profile... [No key binding]

> Run → Profile...

Remove All Breakpoints [No key binding]

> Run → Remove All Breakpoints

Resume [F8]

> Run → Resume

Run Ant Build [Alt+Shift+X, Q]

> Run → Run...

Run Eclipse Application [Alt+Shift+X, E]

> Run → Run...

Run Java Applet [Alt+Shift+X, A]

> Run → Run...

Run Java Application [Alt+Shift+X, J]

> Run → Run...

Run JUnit Plug-in Test [Alt+Shift+X, P]

> Run → Run...

Run JUnit Test [Alt+Shift+X, T]

> Run → Run...

Run Last Launched [Ctrl+F11]

> Run → Run Last Launched

Run Last Launched External Tool [No key binding]

(No menu)

Run SWT Application [Alt+Shift+X, S]

Run → Run...

Run to Line [Ctrl+R]

Run → Run to Line

Run... [No key binding]

Run → Run...

Skip All Breakpoints [No key binding]

Run → Skip All Breakpoints

Step Into [F5]

Run → Step Into

Step Into Selection [Ctrl+F5]

Run → Step Into Selection

Step Over [F6]

Run → Step Over

Step Return [F7]

Run → Step Return

Suspend [No key binding]

Run → Suspend

Terminate [No key binding]

Run → Terminate

Terminate and Relaunch [No key binding]

(No menu)

Toggle Line Breakpoint [Ctrl+Shift+B]

Run → Toggle Line Breakpoint

Toggle Method Breakpoint [No key binding]

    Run → Toggle Method Breakpoint

Toggle Step Filters [Shift+F5]

    Run → Use Step Filters

Toggle Watchpoint [No key binding]

    Run → Toggle Watchpoint

Search Commands

Declaration in Hierarchy [No key binding]

    Search → Declarations → Hierarchy

Declaration in Project [No key binding]

    Search → Declarations → Project

Declaration in Working Set [No key binding]

    Search → Declarations → Working Set…

Declaration in Workspace [Ctrl+G]

    Search → Declarations → Workspace

File Search [No key binding]

    Search → File…

Implementors in Project [No key binding]

    Search → Implementors → Project

Implementors in Working Set [No key binding]

    Search → Implementors → Working Set…

Implementors in Workspace [No key binding]

    Search → Implementors → Workspace

Open Search Dialog [Ctrl+H]

    Search → Search…

Read Access in Hierarchy [No key binding]

  Search → Read Access → Hierarchy

Read Access in Project [No key binding]

  Search → Read Access → Project

Read Access in Working Set [No key binding]

  Search → Read Access → Working Set...

Read Access in Workspace [No key binding]

  Search → Read Access → Workspace

References in Hierarchy [No key binding]

  Search → References → Hierarchy

References in Project [No key binding]

  Search → References → Project

References in Working Set [No key binding]

  Search → References → Working Set...

References in Workspace [Ctrl+Shift+G]

  Search → References → Workspace

Referring Tests [No key binding]

  Search → Referring Tests...

Search All Occurrences in File [No key binding]

  Search → Occurrences in File → Identifier

Search Exception Occurrences in File [No key binding]

  Search → Occurrences in File → Throwing Exception

Search Implement Occurrences in File [No key binding]

  Search → Occurrences in File → Implementing Methods

Show Occurrences in File Quick Menu [Ctrl+Shift+U]

  (No menu)

Write Access in Hierarchy [No key binding]
> Search → Write Access → Hierarchy

Write Access in Project [No key binding]
> Search → Write Access → Project

Write Access in Working Set [No key binding]
> Search → Write Access → Working Set…

Write Access in Workspace [No key binding]
> Search → Write Access → Workspace

Source Commands

Add Block Comment [Ctrl+Shift+/]
> Source → Add Block Comment

Add Constructors from Superclass [No key binding]
> Source → Add Constructors from Superclass…

Add Import [Ctrl+Shift+M]
> Source → Add Import

Add Javadoc Comment [Alt+Shift+J]
> Source → Add Comment

Comment [No key binding]
> (No menu)

Externalize Strings [No key binding]
> Source → Externalize Strings…

Find Strings to Externalize [No key binding]
> Source → Find Strings to Externalize…

Format [Ctrl+Shift+F]
> Source → Format

Format Element [No key binding]

    Source → Format Element

Generate Constructor using Fields [No key binding]

    Source → Generate Constructor using Fields…

Generate Delegate Methods [No key binding]

    Source → Generate Delegate Methods…

Generate Getters and Setters [No key binding]

    Source → Generate Getters and Setters…

Indent Line [Ctrl+I]

    Source → Correct Indentation

Organize Imports [Ctrl+Shift+O]

    Source → Organize Imports

Override/Implement Methods [No key binding]

    Source → Override/Implement Methods…

Quick Assist - Assign parameter to field [No key binding]

    (No menu)

Quick Assist - Assign to field [Ctrl+2, F]

    (No menu)

Quick Assist - Assign to local variable [Ctrl+2, L]

    (No menu)

Quick Assist - Rename in file [Ctrl+2, R]

    (No menu)

Quick Assist - Replace statement with block [No key binding]

    (No menu)

Quick Fix - Add cast [No key binding]

    (No menu)

Quick Fix - Add import [No key binding]

    (No menu)

Quick Fix - Add non-NLS tag [No key binding]

    (No menu)

Quick Fix - Add throws declaration [No key binding]

    (No menu)

Quick Fix - Change to static access [No key binding]

    (No menu)

Quick Fix - Qualify field access [No key binding]

    (No menu)

Remove Block Comment [Ctrl+Shift+\]

    Source → Remove Block Comment

Remove Occurrence Annotations [Alt+Shift+U]

    (No menu)

Show Source Quick Menu [Alt+Shift+S]

    (No menu)

Sort Members [No key binding]

    Source → Sort Members

Surround with try/catch Block [No key binding]

    Source → Surround with try/catch Block

Toggle Comment [Ctrl+/ | Ctrl+7 | Ctrl+Shift+C]

    Source → Toggle Comment

Toggle Mark Occurrences [Alt+Shift+O]

    (No menu)

Uncomment [No key binding]

    (No menu)

Text-Editing Commands

Clear Mark [No key binding]

(No menu)

Collapse [Ctrl+Numpad_Subtract]

(No menu)

Copy Lines [Ctrl+Alt+Down]

(No menu)

Cut Line [No key binding]

(No menu)

Cut to Beginning of Line [No key binding]

(No menu)

Cut to End of Line [No key binding]

(No menu)

Delete Line [Ctrl+D]

(No menu)

Delete Next [Delete]

(No menu)

Delete Next Word [Ctrl+Delete]

(No menu)

Delete Previous [No key binding]

(No menu)

Delete Previous Word [Ctrl+Backspace]

(No menu)

Delete to Beginning of Line [No key binding]

(No menu)

Delete to End of Line [Ctrl+Shift+Delete]

(No menu)

Duplicate Lines [Ctrl+Alt+Up]

(No menu)

Expand [Ctrl+Numpad_Add]

(No menu)

Expand All [Ctrl+Numpad_Multiply]

(No menu)

Insert Line Above Current Line [Ctrl+Shift+Enter]

(No menu)

Insert Line Below Current Line [Shift+Enter]

(No menu)

Line Down [Down]

(No menu)

Line End [End]

(No menu)

Line Start [Home]

(No menu)

Line Up [Up]

(No menu)

Move Lines Down [Alt+Down]

(No menu)

Move Lines Up [Alt+Up]

(No menu)

Next Column [No key binding]

(No menu)

Next Word [Ctrl+Right]

(No menu)

Page Down [Page Down]

(No menu)

Page Up [Page Up]

(No menu)

Previous Column [No key binding]

(No menu)

Previous Word [Ctrl+Left]

(No menu)

Scroll Line Down [Ctrl+Down]

(No menu)

Scroll Line Up [Ctrl+Up]

(No menu)

Select Line Down [Shift+Down]

(No menu)

Select Line End [Shift+End]

(No menu)

Select Line Start [Shift+Home]

(No menu)

Select Line Up [Shift+Up]

(No menu)

Select Next Column [No key binding]

(No menu)

Select Next Word [Ctrl+Shift+Right]

(No menu)

Select Page Down [Shift+Page Down]

(No menu)

Select Page Up [Shift+Page Up]

(No menu)

Select Previous Column [No key binding]

(No menu)

Select Previous Word [Ctrl+Shift+Left]

(No menu)

Select Text End [Ctrl+Shift+End]

(No menu)

Select Text Start [Ctrl+Shift+Home]

(No menu)

Select Window End [No key binding]

(No menu)

Select Window Start [No key binding]

(No menu)

Set Mark [No key binding]

(No menu)

Swap Mark [No key binding]

(No menu)

Text End [Ctrl+End]

(No menu)

Text Start [Ctrl+Home]

(No menu)

To Lower Case [Ctrl+Shift+Y]

(No menu)

To Upper Case [Ctrl+Shift+X]

(No menu)

Toggle Folding [Ctrl+Numpad_Divide]

(No menu)

Toggle Overwrite [Insert]

(No menu)

Window End [No key binding]

(No menu)

Window Start [No key binding]

(No menu)

View Commands

Ant [No key binding]

Window → Show View → Ant

Breakpoints [Alt+Shift+Q, B]

Window → Show View → Breakpoints

Cheat Sheets [Alt+Shift+Q, H]

Window → Show View → Other… → Cheat Sheets → Cheat Sheets

Classic Search [No key binding]

Window → Show View → Other… → Basic → Classic Search

Console [Alt+Shift+Q, C]

Window → Show View → Console

CVS Annotate [No key binding]

Window → Show View → Other… → CVS → CVS Annotate

CVS Editors [No key binding]

Window → Show View → Other… → CVS → CVS Editors

CVS Repositories [No key binding]

Window → Show View → Other… → CVS → CVS Repositories

CVS Resource History [No key binding]

Window → Show View → Other… → CVS → CVS Resource History

Debug [No key binding]

Window → Show View → Debug

Display [No key binding]

Window → Show View → Display

Error Log [No key binding]

Window → Show View → Error Log

Expressions [No key binding]

Window → Show View → Expressions

Java Call Hierarchy [No key binding]

Window → Show View → Other… → Java… → Call Hierarchy

Java Declaration [Alt+Shift+Q, D]

Window → Show View → Declaration

Java Members [No key binding]

Window → Show View → Other… → Java Browsing → Members

Java Package Explorer [Alt+Shift+Q, P]

Window → Show View → Package Explorer

Java Packages [No key binding]

Window → Show View → Other… → Java Browsing → Packages

Java Projects [No key binding]

Window → Show View → Other... → Java Browsing → Projects

Java Type Hierarchy [Alt+Shift+Q, T]

Window → Show View → Hierarchy

Java Types [No key binding]

Window → Show View → Other... → Java Browsing → Types

Javadoc [Alt+Shift+Q, J]

Window → Show View → Javadoc

JUnit [No key binding]

Window → Show View → Other... → Java → JUnit

Memory [No key binding]

Window → Show View → Other... → Debug → Memory

Outline [Alt+Shift+Q, O]

Window → Show View → Outline

Plug-in Dependencies [No key binding]

Window → Show View → Other... → PDE → Plug-in Dependencies

Plug-in Registry [No key binding]

Window → Show View → Other... → PDE Runtime → Registry

Plug-ins [No key binding]

Window → Show View → Other... → PDE → Plug-ins

Problems [Alt+Shift+Q, X]

Window → Show View → Problems

Registers [No key binding]

Window → Show View → Other... → Debug → Registers

Search [Alt+Shift+Q, S]

Window → Show View → Search

Synchronize [Alt+Shift+Q, Y]

Window → Show View → Other… → Team → Synchronize

Variables [Alt+Shift+Q, V]

Window → Show View → Variables

Window Commands

Activate Editor [F12]

Window → Navigation → Activate Editor

Close All Perspectives [No key binding]

Window → Close All Perspectives

Close Perspective [No key binding]

Window → Close Perspective

Customize Perspective [No key binding]

Window → Customize Perspective…

Hide Editors [No key binding]

(No menu)

Lock the Toolbars [No key binding]

(No menu)

Maximize Active View or Editor [Ctrl+M]

Window → Navigation → Maximize Active View or Editor

Minimize Active View or Editor [No key binding]

Window → Navigation → Minimize Active View or Editor

New Editor [No key binding]

Window → New Editor

New Window [No key binding]

Window → New Window

Next Editor [Ctrl+F6]

Window → Navigation → Next Editor

Next Perspective [Ctrl+F8]

Window → Navigation → Next Perspective

Next View [Ctrl+F7]

Window → Navigation → Next View

Open Editor Drop Down [Ctrl+E]

Window → Navigation → Switch to Editor…

Pin Editor [No key binding]

(Available on editor system menu)

Preferences [No key binding]

Window → Preferences…

Previous Editor [Ctrl+Shift+F6]

Window → Navigation → Previous Editor

Previous Perspective [Ctrl+Shift+F8]

Window → Navigation → Previous Perspective

Previous View [Ctrl+Shift+F7]

Window → Navigation → Previous View

Reset Perspective [No key binding]

Window → Reset Perspective

Save Perspective As [No key binding]

Window → Save Perspective As...

Show Key Assist [Ctrl+Shift+L]

Help → Key Assist...

Show Ruler Context Menu [Ctrl+F10]

(No menu)

Show Selected Element Only [No key binding]

(No menu)

Show System Menu [Alt+−]

Window → Navigation → Show System Menu

Show View Menu [Ctrl+F10]

Window → Navigation → Show View Menu

Switch to Editor [Ctrl+Shift+E]

Window → Navigation → Switch to Editor...

Index

We'd like to hear your suggestions for improving our indexes. Send email to
index@oreilly.com.

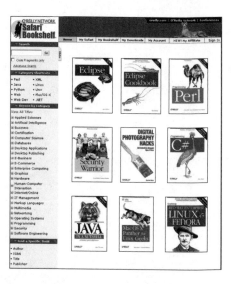